CASE STUDIES IN ATHLETIC TRAINING ADMINISTRATION

Richard Ray, EdD, ATC
Hope College
Holland, Michigan

Human Kinetics

Library of Congress Cataloging-in-Publication Data

Ray, Richard, 1957-
   Case studies in athletic training administration / Richard Ray.
      p.   cm.
   ISBN 0-87322-675-5
   1. Physical education and training--Administration--Case studies.
   2. Athletic trainers--Training of--Case studies.   I. Title.
   GV343.5.R39   1995
   796'.06'9--dc20   94-28362
                                                                  CIP

ISBN: 0-87322-675-5

Acquisitions Editor: Rick Frey, PhD; **Developmental Editor:** Judy Patterson
Wright, PhD; **Assistant Editors:** Ed Giles and Hank Woolsey; **Copyeditor:**
Ginger Rodriguez; **Proofreader:** Pam Johnson; **Typesetter and Text Layout:**
Julie Overholt; **Text Designer:** Judy Henderson; **Cover Designer:** Keith Blomb-
erg; **Printer:** United Graphics

Printed in the United States of America   10   9   8   7   6   5   4   3   2   1

Human Kinetics
P.O. Box 5076, Champaign, IL 61825-5076
1-800-747-4457

Canada: Human Kinetics, Box 24040, Windsor, ON N8Y 4Y9
1-800-465-7301 (in Canada only)

Europe: Human Kinetics, P.O. Box IW14, Leeds LS16 6TR, England
(44) 532 781708

Australia: Human Kinetics, Unit 5, 32 Raglan Avenue,
Edwardstown, South Australia
(08) 371 3755

New Zealand: Human Kinetics, P.O. Box 105-231, Auckland 1
(09) 309 2259

For Sean

Contents

Preface

The body of knowledge in athletic training continues to grow unabated, and many of us find it difficult to keep pace with all of the new developments in our field. Although this challenge is most noticeable in the job domains requiring clinical knowledge and skill, many athletic trainers recognize that the quality of their job performance and the level of their job satisfaction depends to an increasing degree on their managerial skills. Our ability to be visionary leaders who can confront administrative problems and develop creative solutions is a significant factor in our perceived effectiveness.

This book is the second step in teaching you the managerial concepts you need to function effectively in a sports medicine market of growing complexity. Step 1, the book *Management Strategies in Athletic Training* (see the order form at the end of this book for more information), is important, but athletic trainers need even more preparation in this area. Managerial skill depends not only on learning administrative concepts and retaining facts, but also on something much more elusive and difficult to teach—the ability to think critically. Even those who can quote chapter and verse on managerial theory will be ineffective administrators if they cannot analyze a problem, develop a list of solutions, weigh their benefits, and implement a plan of action. This book is intended to help you develop and practice these important skills.

The case study method of instruction has been used effectively for years across a wide variety of disciplines. Most instructors of courses in athletic training administration use anecdotes from their experiences or those of others to bring life to managerial concepts that can seem abstract to the uninitiated. *Case Studies in Athletic Training Administration* will help provide breadth and structure to this valuable teaching practice. The 30 cases are drawn primarily from real-life situations faced by athletic trainers in every conceivable practice setting. If you are an athletic training educator, this new learning tool will let you present a broader perspective to your students. If you are a student, you will receive important exposure to actual administrative problems before being forced to confront such issues in the "real world."

There are two primary audiences for this text:

- Undergraduate and graduate students preparing for degrees in athletic training and for credentialing by national and local standard-setting boards
- Athletic trainers charged with preparing student athletic trainers for certification, licensing, and the world of work in sports medicine

This text can be used by itself or in conjunction with *Management Strategies in Athletic Training* or other textbooks in athletic training administration. Its 30 cases describe administrative problems faced by athletic trainers in high school, college, and professional athletics; hospital and private sports medicine clinics; industrial settings; and athletic training education settings. The 30 cases are presented in random order. The grid on page ix will help you locate cases that deal with a specific setting or administrative concept. Each case has enough detail so you can understand the setting and develop alternative strategies for resolving the problem. A series of analysis questions after each case helps you formulate strategies to resolve the case. Most importantly, they challenge you to think about how the problem might have been avoided, helping you become proactive rather than reactive in your role as an athletic trainer–administrator. The questions are intentionally open ended and unaccompanied by canned answers. Think as creatively and broadly as possible in developing alternative strategies. Managerial problems rarely have only one solution; most have many—some better than others.

If you are an athletic training educator, you can use this book to improve your students' critical thinking skills in several ways. First, the cases can generate spirited class discussion. The variety of opinions your students express (and the tenacity with which they express them) as they respond to the case questions may surprise you. Using this text in classroom discussion helps your students not only apply the managerial concepts they have learned, but also clarify their values for relating to people in problem situations. Your careful guidance of this process will be one of the greatest gifts you can give your students.

The case studies also can be used as homework. Focusing attention outside of class on applying managerial concepts in actual practice settings can be a valuable adjunct to classroom learning. An application exercise is provided for each case study. The application exercises are designed to encourage readers to take concrete, proactive measures to help avoid the problems presented in the case. A cross-reference to the *Management Strategies in Athletic Training* book is located at the end of each case study so you can acquire more information on the concepts presented in the specific case study.

Finally, you may find some of the case studies appropriate as examination questions. This approach has been demonstrated to challenge students' higher order thinking skills in ways that more traditional examinations cannot.

Whether you are a student, an educator, or a practicing athletic trainer interested in improving your grasp of administration, I am confident that you will find *Case Studies in Athletic Training Administration* a new and exciting means for achieving mastery in sports medicine management.

Setting by Concept Grid of Case Studies

Use this chart as a guide to locate the number of a particular case study according to the setting and the concept(s) illustrated.

*Concept / Setting	Program planning	Human resources	Policy and procedures	Communication	Information management	Legal liability	Financial management	Facility planning	Ethics
High school	2, 9, 19	19, 22	1, *9, 12, *19, *22	*1, 2, 19, 22	*12	1, 9, 12, 19, 22	*2, 9		12
College	3, 8, 10, 17	*3, *5, *13	3, *10, 18, *21, 24, 28	5, 8, *28	*18, 28	3, 13, 21, *24, 28	*17	*8	21, 24, 28
College athletic training educator		4	4, 20						*4, *20
Professional athletics	6		6	6	*6				
Clinical	7, *15, 23, *29	15, 25, 26, 30	15, *23, 26, *30	15	*26, 27	23, 25, 27, 30	*7, 15, 23, 26, 27, 29	7	*25, *27, 30
Industrial	*11	11		11, 16	16	*16			11
High school/clinical		*14		14					

*Asterisk denotes primary concept illustrated in a specific case study.

Note to Instructors

Many of us use examples—anecdotes, stories, and other tales—from our own experience when teaching our students about athletic training administration. "I remember the time when . . ." is a frequent phrase for most of us. This practice is the most basic form of the case study method of teaching. Although it plays an important role in helping students learn about the administrative issues and problems faced in athletic training and in passing along the culture of our profession, the technique fails one crucial test required for student learning: *discovery*. I hope that through using a more formalized approach to the class study method you will help your students examine these stories in the sometimes harsh light of critical analysis.

▌ What Is a Case Study?

As early as 1953, this teaching tool was described by Paul Lawrence:[1]

> *A good case is the vehicle by which a chunk of reality is brought into the classroom to be worked over by the class and the instructor. A good case keeps the class discussion grounded upon some of the stubborn facts that must be faced in real life situations. It is the anchor on academic flights of speculation. It is the record of complex situations that must be literally pulled apart and put together again for the expression of attitudes or ways of thinking brought into the classroom. (p. 215)*

The case method of instruction is grounded in the discovery, evaluation, and critical assessment of various solutions to a problem. This is usually

---

▌ [1]Lawrence, P. (1953). The preparation of case material. In K.R. Andrews (Ed.), *The case method of teaching human relations and administration*. Cambridge, MA: Harvard University Press.

accomplished through discussion among students facilitated by an instructor who understands the likely consequences of the assorted responses. Your task is to draw students into meaningful dialogue on the critical elements of each of the cases in this text. The analysis questions at the end of each case are provided as aids. They are not an exhaustive source of inquiry, but rather a guide to the major concepts of the case. To provide an idea of the type of analysis that can be accomplished using this method, I have "answered" the questions following the first case for you by developing various solutions to the problem. You should also consider developing a list of discussion questions to stimulate classroom dialogue among students. The level of analysis you choose for each case should be based on a number of factors, including these:

- Your values regarding the various elements of the case
- Your estimate of the students' values regarding the various elements of the case
- Your level of experience and knowledge in the subject of the case
- The students' level of experience and knowledge in the subject of the case

∎ Instructor as Facilitator

If you teach using the lecture method, you will undoubtedly find your role as discussion facilitator in the case method of instruction challenging. Often, the most difficult task is getting the discussion rolling and headed in the right direction. Frederick (1980) offers the following suggestions to help you accomplish this part of your task:[2]

- Ask students to pair off, discuss the value of the case in meeting the objectives of the course, and then present their findings to the class.
- Ask students to take turns restating the facts of the case while you list them on the board.
- Ask students to generate their own questions to analyze the case.
- Ask individual students to read aloud the portion of the case they feel is most significant and to explain why it is important.
- Break the class into small groups to discuss a particular aspect of a case. Ask each group to report on its discussion and analysis.

∎ [2]Frederick, P. (1980). The dreaded discussion: Ten ways to start. *Improving College and University Teaching*, **29**(3), 109-114.

- Challenge individuals or groups of students to generate "truth statements" about a few of the major issues in a case. These statements should represent the truth as a student understands it, for example, "Bidding is the best way to purchase supplies" or "Excess insurance is the most appropriate form of athletic injury insurance for schools." Allow other students to challenge these statements.
- Assign predefined positions and stage debates between students.
- Assign students the identities of various characters in the case and ask them to role play.
- Provide an agenda for discussion and then withdraw from the conversation, allowing students to direct the analysis of the case.
- Once the students are experienced in the discussion method, simply ask them how they liked the case and see where the discussion goes.

Finally, always remember that the case method of instruction is only that—a method. It does not take the place of mastering administrative concepts and theories in more traditional ways. It does not make out-of-classroom reading, library work, and homework obsolete by replacing them with in-class discussion. The analysis questions are valuable to help improve your students' critical thinking skills, especially when used in conjunction with the application exercises. As such, the case method should become an important tool in your personal arsenal of teaching skills. I hope it will result in a new generation of athletic trainers better prepared to take on the increasingly complex administrative challenges they are sure to face.

Acknowledgments

The cases in this book are the real-life experiences of a diverse group of athletic trainers. I am grateful to the following friends for sharing their stories:

Ronnie Barnes, ATC
New York Giants
East Rutherford, NJ

Robert Behnke, HSD, ATC
Indiana State University
Terre Haute, IN

Gerald Bell, EdD, ATC
University of Illinois
Urbana-Champaign, IL

Lynn Bott, ATC
University of Kansas
Lawrence, KS

Scott Bruce, ATC
Slippery Rock State University
Slippery Rock, PA

Kirk Brumels, ATC
New England Patriots
Foxboro, MA

Lorin Cartwright, ATC
Pioneer High School
Ann Arbor, MI

Marty Daniel, ATC
Walbro Corporation
Cass City, MI

Kent Falb, ATC
Detroit Lions
Pontiac, MI

Connie Grauer, ATC
University of Kansas
Lawrence, KS

Joe Harbottle, ATC
Dykstra Libby Physical Therapy
Holland, MI

Gary Howe, ATC
Holland Community Hospital
Holland, MI

Deb Kiekover, ATC
West Ottawa High School
Holland, MI

Robert Moss, PhD, ATC
Western Michigan University
Kalamazoo, MI

Frank Randall, ATC
Iowa State University
Ames, IA

Brian Razak, ATC
Fort Hays State University
Hays, KS

Joe Recknagel, ATC
Detroit Lions
Pontiac, MI

Cyndy Stannard, ATC
American Rehab Network
Southgate, MI

Marty Richards, ATC
Upper Iowa University
Fayette, IA

. . . and several others who wished to remain anonymous.

I am also indebted to Hope College for its support of this project. Finally, I want to thank the professionals at Human Kinetics, especially Rick Frey and Judy Patterson Wright, for their guidance and counsel.

CASE STUDY 1

■ **Topic:** Dealing with "helpful" parents

■ **Setting:** High school

■ **Primary concept:** Communication

■ **Secondary concepts:** Policy and procedure development
Legal liability

James Spellman was as excited as the girls on the Martin Luther King High School gymnastics team when the bus pulled into the university arena parking lot to drop the team off for its final practice before the state championship meet. MLK had a great tradition in gymnastics. When James arrived 2 years earlier as the school's first athletic trainer, he was swept up by the pride and school spirit generated for the team and its success. When the coach invited him to accompany the team to the state championship meet, he jumped at the chance.

When the team walked into the huge arena, they were surprised to see a large contingent of classmates and parents who had come to watch them practice. Most of the girls went to the locker room to change for practice, while James used the bleachers as a makeshift taping table for several athletes.

While James was taping, a parent of one of the athletes, Dr. John Russell, walked over to strike up a conversation. Dr. Russell, whose daughter was a freshman, was a thorn in James's side. Dr. Russell, a dermatologist, desperately wanted to become a team physician for the school. Although James appreciated the willingness to help, the school's sports medicine program was already served by a family practitioner and an orthopedic surgeon, both of whom devoted a significant part of their professional practice and continuing education to sports medicine. James felt he had an ideal situation, and he wanted nothing to jeopardize it. Unfortunately, Dr. Russell had interjected himself into more than one case involving a gymnastics injury. Although James's initial instinct had been to ask Dr. Russell to keep out of the situation, he kept silent for several reasons. Dr. Russell was a powerful figure in the medical community, and James didn't want to be on his bad side. James also hoped that with time Dr. Russell would "see the light" and back off. Finally, James knew that as a practical matter his athletes had the right to select any physician of their choice.

The next day during the beam competition, one of the MLK athletes slipped during her dismount and landed hard on her lumbosacral spine. James was nearby and immediately began to evaluate her injury. As he was doing so, Dr. Russell rushed out of the stands to the scene of the injury, where he began to conduct his own assessment. "We've got to do something about these lumbar spasms," proclaimed Dr. Russell. Before the flabbergasted James could react, Dr. Russell began passively flexing the athlete's hips by slowly forcing her knees to her chest. "Dr. Russell," James said, "I really think we should avoid moving her. The mechanism of injury, muscle spasm, pain, and the tingling in her legs could indicate a spinal injury." "Don't worry," Dr. Russell responded, "I know what I'm doing."

After it became clear that the athlete's back pain was not resolving, James called an ambulance. X rays taken at the university hospital revealed a compression fracture of L4.

▌ Analysis Questions

1. What is the primary management concept illustrated through this case?

Alternative 1

The primary concept is communication between the various members of the sports medicine program and major outside interests. Dr. Russell represents a major outside interest whose beliefs and actions could affect the program in significant ways. James's failure to creatively manage Dr. Russell's enthusiasm for the program while communicating support for the role of his two team physicians was a critical error and should be taken as the most important lesson of this case.

Alternative 2

The primary concept is the need to have formal policies, processes, and procedures that support the mission of the sports medicine program. If MLK High School had an appropriate policy that defined the school board's position on the use of consultants, supported by written procedures specific to the sports medicine program, James's position relative to Dr. Russell could have been clarified greatly. He would have been able to tell Dr. Russell in specific terms why he could not allow him to work with the high school's athletes, and he would have been positioned to receive direct support from his superiors if Dr. Russell failed to comply with the policy.

Alternative 3

The main thing to be learned from this case is the danger of legal liability if an emergency plan is not in place to guide the actions of the athletic trainer. Because James had no emergency plan for dealing with an athlete's injury, his actions could be dictated by an outside force. Although an emergency plan cannot address every possible situation, the kind of injury that James faced was of such a routine nature that an emergency plan would have gone a long way toward avoiding the legal mess he could now find himself in.

2. Who runs the greatest risk of legal liability in this case?

Alternative 1

As the legal representative of the school board, James Spellman had the greatest legal responsibility to properly care for the injured athlete. James was the only person present at the meet who had a legal duty to provide assistance. This duty was presumably created and codified in both his employment contract and his position description. Hence, James had the greatest responsibility to ensure that the injured athlete received the proper care. If anyone should be concerned about the legal consequences of this injury, it is James Spellman.

Alternative 2

Dr. Russell is likely to suffer the greatest legal consequences because he is the person who actually rendered the care that may have aggravated the athlete's injury. Beyond this irrefutable fact, he is the health care practitioner who will be held to the highest standard of care. Even if he attempts to use a Good Samaritan legal defense, he should be concerned because such a defense does not protect against wanton or willful negligence.

Alternative 3

The school board is the only entity that has any real legal problems as a result of the way this case was handled. The reasons are fairly obvious: The board has the "deepest pockets," which will make it the first target of any sensible prosecuting attorney. The body of case law that supports the legal responsibility of school boards to provide both a safe environment for participation and reasonable medical care for injured students is well established. Finally, even though the board had a formal relationship with two physicians, neither were required to be in attendance at the meet. Had one of them been required to attend, the situation presumably would have been handled in a manner more consistent with the standard of care for such injuries.

Alternative 4

The threat of serious legal consequences is minimal in this case. The compression fracture of L4 was undoubtedly caused by the fall the athlete experienced, not by the first aid rendered by either James or Dr. Russell. Assuming there were no serious side effects from the attempts to reduce the athlete's lumbar spasm—which is a fairly safe assumption because most lumbar compression fractures are relatively stable—the athlete would have a difficult time arguing that she had suffered any damage as a result of the treatment.

3. How would you have acted differently if you were in James's position?

Alternative 1

James should have told Dr. Russell to keep away from his athletes the first time he attempted to interfere with a case, both in direct conversation and in a letter James could use to protect himself against any adverse consequences of Dr. Russell's behavior. Although James should have been polite, he also should have been very firm to prevent any confusion about Dr. Russell's role.

Alternative 2

James should have enlisted the assistance of his two team physicians to discourage Dr. Russell as soon as he realized Dr. Russell could be a problem. As professional colleagues of equal standing in the community, their influence would have been greater than James's. Dr. Russell obviously felt he could ignore James's feelings about participating in athlete care. He would have probably thought twice about incurring the wrath of two of his professional colleagues, however.

Alternative 3

James should have welcomed Dr. Russell's obvious enthusiasm for the program from the beginning. If he had channeled Dr. Russell's desire to become involved in the MLK sports medicine program in a positive direction, he would have been less likely to find himself in an adversarial relationship with Dr. Russell at the gymnastics meet. If James had encouraged Dr. Russell to consult more frequently with his other two team physicians, Dr. Russell may have improved his knowledge of sports medicine. In addition, he probably would have been more receptive to James's advice at the injury scene.

▌ Application Exercise*

Write a fictional letter to Dr. Russell explaining James's concerns in this matter. Assume that you are writing the letter *before* the incident at the state meet. See pp. 6-7 for two sample letters.

▌ **Note to readers*: The application exercises at the end of each case are designed to encourage you to take concrete, proactive measures to help avoid the problems presented in the case.

▌ For background information on concepts presented in Case Study 1, see *Management Strategies in Athletic Training*, chapters 2 and 8.

Sample Letter 1

Dr. John Russell, M.D.
204 Oak Street
Big City, MI 48000

Dear Dr. Russell:

It was good to see you at the gymnastics meet yesterday. I always enjoy spending time in conversation with our athletes' parents—especially when we can discuss sports medicine!

Dr. Russell, even though you and I enjoy a fine relationship—one I definitely want to preserve and enhance—I need to express an important concern. As you know, there have been a couple of injuries on the gymnastics team that you have chosen to involve yourself with this year. Although I know you were motivated by a genuine sense of concern for the injured athletes, your involvement in these cases led to some confusion on the part of the athletes, their parents, and our team physicians. Being a parent yourself, I'm sure you are aware of the tremendous effort we have made to educate both athletes and their parents regarding our sports medicine policies and procedures. One of the procedures we have worked the hardest to communicate is the requirement that all injured athletes be referred either to one of our team physicians or to the athlete's family physician. I'm sure you can see how your involvement in these cases hinders our ability to implement these procedures.

Dr. Russell, I'm sure that you can still play an important role in our sports medicine program. There are many instances during the year when we require the services of an excellent dermatologist like you. I must ask, however, that you limit your involvement to those cases referred to you by one of our team physicians. I hope you understand my concerns and that we can continue to work together as professional colleagues and friends.

Thanks again for your unwavering support of both our program and our school. We need more parents like you! Please feel free to give me a call if you want to discuss this matter in more detail. In any case, I look forward to seeing you at the state meet in two weeks.

With Warmest Regards,

James Spellman, ATC
Head Athletic Trainer

Sample Letter 2

Dr. John Russell, M.D.
204 Oak Street
Big City, MI 48000

Dear Dr. Russell:

The purpose of this letter is to express my concern over your un-invited and unwanted involvement in the medical care of injured MLK High School student-athletes. There have been several times during the past year when you have involved yourself in the medical care of our athletes without following the chain of medical command as established by the MLK administration and endorsed by the Board of Education. As you may know, all injured student-athletes must be medically authorized to play by one of MLK's team physicians. When you jump into a case without being asked, you upset the procedures we have worked so hard to develop over the years. The result is a confused student-athlete and team physicians who are upset because they feel they are being second guessed by someone with no training or expertise in sports medicine.

Please accept my thanks for your enthusiastic support of our school, but please honor my request to leave the medical care of our student-athletes to our team physicians.

Sincerely,

James Spellman, ATC
Head Athletic Trainer

cc: Angela Tomlinson, Athletic Director
*   Bruce McDonald, Team Physician*
*   Delbert Delany, Superintendent of Schools*

CASE STUDY 2

■ **Topic:**   Budgeting during hard times

■ **Setting:**   High school

■ **Primary concept:**   Financial management

■ **Secondary concepts:**   Program planning and evaluation
Communication

When Sharon Carpenter finished adding up the numbers for the third time, she knew she had a problem. The athletic director at the high school where she worked as an athletic trainer had told her a few weeks earlier that a freshman football team would be added to the athletic program next year. Unfortunately, he also told her that her budget would not be increased. "It's possible," he added, "that we may even have to decrease your budget and a few other budgets to pay for the new team. I'm sorry about this Sharon, but I don't know what else to do."

Sharon was at her wit's end. Her budget for athletic training supplies and services was already inadequate. She was very frugal, however, and she had found many creative ways to stretch her budget in the past. The new team and its effect on her budget, however, would significantly impact her ability to provide even the most basic services to her student-athletes.

Although Sharon knew she could end up in trouble, she decided to do something about the ridiculous budget situation. She called the school superintendent and gave him the full history of her budget problems. She explained how this new freshman football program would ruin her program in the absence of additional funding. The superintendent was surprised to hear this. "Didn't anybody over there tell you about the new budgeting system we're implementing?" he asked. "Every budgetary unit of the school system, including yours, will be required to develop a zero-based budget for next year. The budget must list every item and service you wish to purchase and include a detailed rationale indicating why the purchase is necessary. After the school district finance office evaluates your requests, your budget will be set for next year. It's possible that your budget could even go up if you can do a good job justifying each expense.''

Sharon was relieved to learn that her budget could still be salvaged. She knew she had a lot of work to do, however, so she decided to begin right away.

▌ Analysis Questions

1. Would you have gone over the athletic director to the school superintendent if you were in Sharon's position? Why or why not?

2. What alternatives did Sharon have under the circumstances? What are the risks and benefits of each alternative?

3. What risks are involved in circumventing your supervisor's authority? How should you decide if the possible benefits are worth the risks?

▌ Application Exercise

Develop a zero-based budget for Sharon's program. Include both goods and services. Assume the following program variables:

- 500 student-athletes in 22 sports, including varsity, junior varsity, and freshman football, and gymnastics and wrestling
- Five student athletic trainers who the program has traditionally sent to summer athletic training workshops
- A training room that contains well-maintained equipment consistent with most high school sports medicine programs
- Low inventory levels for most consumable supplies
- School district policy that requires competitive bidding on items over $300

▌ For background information on concepts presented in Case Study 2, see *Management Strategies in Athletic Training*, chapters 1 and 4.

CASE STUDY 3

▌**Topic:** Gender and racial considerations for hiring

▌**Setting:** College

▌**Primary concept:** Human resources

▌**Secondary concepts:** Program planning and evaluation
Policy and procedure development
Legal liability

Harold White was the head athletic trainer at Northwest A & M. A few months ago he was informed that his top assistant was leaving the university to take a head trainer job at another league school. Although Harold was happy for his assistant, he dreaded having to go through all the work of hiring a new assistant.

Harold placed advertisements in the *NCAA News* and *The Chronicle of Higher Education* and on the computerized job bulletin board of the National Athletic Trainers Association. He received more than 100 applications for the position. After sorting out the applications according to years of experience and type of previous employment setting, he conducted telephone interviews with the top 10 candidates. Then he narrowed the list to his top three choices. When he went to the athletic director for permission to bring the candidates to campus for on-site interviews, the AD told him that he thought the list looked pretty good, but that Harold needed approval from the university's affirmative action officer first. Harold wasn't happy about having to deal with what he considered an extra layer of bureaucracy, but he knew he had to "play the game" to get his assistant hired. He sent the three files over to the affirmative action office.

Three days later Harold met with the affirmative action officer to discuss the candidates. "Mr. White," she began, "we have a problem here. First, in reviewing your current staff I discovered that every member of your sports medicine program is a white male. That is a problem all by itself given the university president's mandate of 2 years ago to bring greater gender and racial balance to our faculty and staff. Then there is the matter of these applicants, who are also white males. The reason I know these candidates are white males is because you asked them to attach a photo of themselves to their applications, which is a serious violation of state and university hiring policies. I'm sorry, Mr. White, but I cannot approve these candidates. Furthermore, I will not approve any candidate until you can demonstrate a commitment to diversity in your program. I suggest you go back through your applications or readvertise. Do not send me any additional candidates until you have prepared a long-range hiring plan that will eventually result in gender balance within your staff and that also addresses the issue of racial inclusiveness."

Harold was frustrated and angry. After all, it wasn't his fault that the most qualified applicants were white. He was willing to consider nonwhite candidates, but none had applied. Was he to blame for that? He wanted to hire a female at some point, but the person who took this position would have to work with the football program, and he didn't think the football coaches would approve of a female athletic trainer. He wasn't sure what to do.

▮ Analysis Questions

1. What staff recruitment process would you have used if you were in Harold's position? What flaws, if any, exist in the methods that Harold used?

2. What strategies could Harold consider to create greater racial and gender balance on his staff?

▮ Application Exercise

Develop a long-range hiring plan for Harold's program according to the guidelines described by the affirmative action officer. Assume the following:

- Harold has a staff of four full-time assistants and two graduate assistants.
- All assistants are under age 35.
- The assistants' average length of employment is 5 years.
- Staff size is fixed.

■ For background information on concepts presented in Case Study 3, see *Management Strategies in Athletic Training*, chapters 2, 3, and 8.

CASE STUDY 4

∎ **Topic:** Romantic relationships with clients

∎ **Setting:** College athletic training educator

∎ **Primary concept:** Ethics

∎ **Secondary concepts:** Human resources
Policy and procedure development

Ron was a 23-year-old assistant athletic trainer at the university. In addition to his duties as athletic trainer for the soccer and track programs, he was also a clinical instructor in the accredited athletic training curriculum. Jenny was a 21-year-old junior on the university's track team, majoring in athletic training.

During the winter term of Ron's first year on the job, he was assigned to teach the therapeutic modalities course to the athletic training majors. He was pleasantly surprised to learn that Jenny was a student in the class. He didn't know her very well, but he had met her once or twice in the training room. Jenny was smart, pretty, and well liked. Although Ron wasn't ready to admit it, he was attracted to her.

One day during the indoor track season, Jenny approached the high-jump pit, planted her foot, and felt a popping sensation in her knee. She collapsed to the ground in pain. Ron attended to her injury by implementing the appropriate first aid procedures and referred her to the team orthopedic surgeon. The physician diagnosed the problem as an isolated tear of the anterior cruciate ligament and recommended reconstructive surgery. Jenny was confused and upset about the injury and the prospect of surgery, so she sought out Ron's advice. Ron patiently and professionally explained the physician's recommendation and described the rehabilitation that

Jenny would go through after the surgery. Jenny felt better after the talk and decided to proceed with the operation, which was scheduled in 3 weeks.

Jenny began her preoperative course of rehabilitation the next day. She and Ron saw each other every day for rehabilitation and every other day for therapeutic modalities class. Ron's attraction to Jenny grew stronger with each day and it seemed to him that Jenny might be attracted to him as well. A week before the surgery, Ron asked Jenny out on a date. Jenny accepted immediately. Over the course of the next few months, their relationship grew until it was known throughout the department that Ron and Jenny were a couple.

▌ Analysis Questions

1. Is it ethical for Ron to have a romantic relationship with Jenny? Why or why not? What are the potential pitfalls inherent in this type of relationship?

2. Would your response to question 1 above be different if Ron were not Jenny's instructor? If he were not Jenny's athletic trainer?

3. Is the fact that Jenny apparently entered the relationship of her own free will and without coercion relevant to this case?

4. Would your responses to any of the questions above be different if Ron were 43 instead of 23? If Jenny were the athletic trainer/clinical instructor and Ron the student?

5. What are the policy implications for the sports medicine program in this case? For the athletic training curriculum? For the university?

▌ Application Exercise

Assume that you are Ron's supervising athletic trainer and director of the athletic training curriculum. Outline a strategy for handling this case.

Consider using your university's or program's policies and procedures to guide your actions. If none exist, draft your own. Specify each step you would take, and outline the possible responses to your actions. If you would choose to take no action in this case, defend your decision by outlining a hypothetical conversation with Jenny's angry father.

■ For background information on concepts presented in Case Study 4, see *Management Strategies in Athletic Training*, chapters 1 and 2.

CASE STUDY 5

■ **Topic:** Working through professional differences

■ **Setting:** College

■ **Primary concept:** Human resources

■ **Secondary concept:** Communication

Dan Jones had worked hard over the past 4 years to build a sports medicine program that was the envy of many small college athletic trainers around the country. He had developed an excellent relationship with the college's administration, which was something his predecessor had failed to accomplish. A solid core of student athletic trainers was being successfully prepared for certification. His budget was adequate to support program needs, and the new training room was state of the art.

The only major problem Dan had yet to solve was that of his team physician. Dr. Barton Huxley was 60 years old and had practiced all of his professional life in the small town that was home to the college. He was a general practitioner, which was his one redeeming feature because it meant he was adept at treating the many medical conditions that Dan's athletes developed. Dr. Huxley's orthopedic skills, unfortunately, left much to be desired. He was extremely conservative. For example, Dr. Huxley's common practice was to place a first-degree medial collateral ligament (MCL) sprain in a full-leg plaster cast for 3 weeks before allowing the athlete to begin a rehabilitation program. When he did refer orthopedic problems, he usually sent the college's athletes to a group of equally conservative orthopedists in the next town, even though a fine orthopedic specialist with a genuine interest and expertise in sports injury care had just moved into town.

The coaches took out their frustrations on Dan when he told them how long their athletes would be out with injuries, and Dan was frustrated himself—especially because he knew that Dr. Huxley had been the team physician at the college for nearly 30 years, served on the college's board of trustees, and was a generous contributor to the annual fund.

One day Dan decided that he had to take some action. He went down to the AD's office and explained the problem in full detail. The AD nodded knowingly, smiled, and said, "Dan, I understand your problem. Some of the coaches have complained to me about Dr. Huxley as well. But you need to understand something, son. Dr. Barton Huxley is very important to this college and he *will* remain our team physician until the day he voluntarily decides he wants to retire."

▮ Analysis Questions

1. Prior to approaching the AD, what alternative actions should Dan have considered? Which of the alternatives would you have pursued? Why?

2. Now that Dan has spoken with the AD, is he stuck with Dr. Huxley, or are there any other options he can pursue? What are the risks of pursuing those options?

3. What allies might Dan attempt to enlist in his effort to obtain a new team physician? How could he use the allies?

4. Once Dr. Huxley finally retires or is replaced, what strategies should Dan consider when choosing a new team physician to avoid the problems he faced with Dr. Huxley?

▮ Application Exercise

Assign a fellow student or colleague to play the role of Dr. Huxley while you play the part of Dan. Pretend that you have invited Dr. Huxley to lunch and that you use the opportunity to discuss your concerns with him. What will you say? How will he respond? Analyze the conversation afterward to predict its effect on your relationship and your program.

▮ For background information on concepts presented in Case Study 5, see *Management Strategies in Athletic Training*, chapters 1 and 3.

CASE STUDY 6

∎ **Topic:**   Developing a priority for information

∎ **Setting:**   Professional athletics

∎ **Primary concept:**   Information management

∎ **Secondary concepts:**   Program planning and evaluation
Policy and procedure development
Communication

Buck Martin, the right fielder for the local minor league baseball team, tracked the ball as soon as it came off the bat. He turned and sprinted back toward the warning track while shielding his eyes from the sun that was beginning to dip below the grandstand roof. With a mighty leap, Buck reached for the ball just as the left side of his body crashed into the unpadded brick wall that served as an outfield fence in the ancient ballpark. Buck abandoned all thought of catching the ball as pain seared through his left shoulder, and he fell to the ground, obviously injured. The team's athletic trainer, Mike Vincent, raced out to right field to survey the damage. Mike's cursory examination on the field revealed a prominent bump near the tip of Buck's left shoulder. After Buck regained his composure, Mike walked him back to the dugout so the team physician, a local family practitioner who loved baseball, could diagnose the problem. ''It looks like you may have separated your shoulder, Buck,'' said the physician. ''Mike, make an appointment for Buck with one of the orthopedists. Let's see what they have to say.''

The next morning Mike called the local orthopedic office and arranged for Buck to be seen later that day. Unfortunately, the team was leaving for a weekend road trip in about an hour, so Mike would not be able to accompany Buck to the doctor's office as he usually would. Mike told Buck to follow the doctor's orders and he would see him in a few days.

The team did not return from the road trip until about 4:00 a.m. Monday, and Mike decided to grab a little extra sleep when he got home. At about 9:00, he was jarred awake by the phone. "Mike, this is Coach Perkins. Sorry to call you at home, but it's been nearly 4 days and you still haven't told me the status of Buck Martin. Now, Mike, I need to know how long this thing is going to keep him out. If he won't be able to play, I've got to get on the horn and dig up another player from somewhere." "Coach," replied Mike, "give me an hour and I'll call you back and let you know."

Mike tried calling Buck at his apartment, but there was no response. He threw on some clothes and went over to the diner where many of the players often ate breakfast, and he found Buck and his girlfriend drinking coffee. When Mike asked Buck what the doctor had told him about his shoulder, Buck told him that he really didn't understand everything the doctor had said. "Something about a C joint and a sprained rotation cuff," muttered a dejected Buck. Mike knew he wasn't going to get any useful information from Buck, so he decided to call the orthopedist. Unfortunately, the receptionist informed him that the doctor was involved in two major surgical cases in the morning and was flying out to an international conference on arthroscopy in the afternoon. It was very unlikely he would be able to return Mike's phone call until after he returned from the conference.

Mike was frustrated at not knowing the status of one of his team's best players. With a sense of foreboding he began to dial the phone to let the coach know that it would be a while before he knew anything more about Buck's shoulder.

∎ Analysis Questions

1. If you were in Mike Vincent's position, how would you have handled this injury in order to get the information you needed in a timely manner?

2. What options, if any, could Mike exercise to get the information he needs after the receptionist told him the doctor wouldn't be able to

get back to him right away? Are there any risks involved in exercising those options?

∎ Application Exercise

Design a medical referral system that would help Mike avoid problems like this in the future. Be sure to include any appropriate policies to justify the practices you outline.

∎ For background information on concepts presented in Case Study 6, see *Management Strategies in Athletic Training*, chapters 2 and 6.

CASE STUDY 7

■ **Topic:** Purchasing a private practice

■ **Setting:** Clinical

■ **Primary concept:** Financial management

■ **Secondary concepts:** Program planning and evaluation
Facility planning

Taylor King, ATC, PT, had worked for Johnson Physical Therapy Services for 5 years when Eric Johnson called her into his office and announced that he was retiring. Furthermore, he wanted Taylor to purchase the business. Although Taylor was honored that Eric Johnson wanted her to carry on with the practice, she had several concerns. First, she would have to borrow nearly $100,000 to purchase the clinic. Although she had about $10,000 of equity built up in her house, she still had very little in her savings account because she had just finished paying off her college and PT school loans. The other concern was that she had a strong desire to expand the practice by doing more sports medicine outreach, both with the local high schools and with the community in general. To do that she needed at least two more treatment rooms and a rehabilitation gymnasium. She would have to expand the clinic, increasing the amount she would have to borrow even more.

Despite all the uncertainties, Taylor felt that this was a great opportunity to own her own clinic. She wasn't sure when or if another opportunity like it would come along. After thinking about it for a few days, Taylor informed Eric Johnson that she would like to purchase the practice contingent on her ability to secure a loan from the bank.

▌Analysis Questions

1. What factors would you consider if you were in Taylor's position when trying to decide if you should purchase the clinic? Where would you look for help in answering your questions?

2. How should Taylor develop her idea to bring more sports medicine business to Johnson Physical Therapy Services? Who should she target? How should she do it? Develop a marketing plan for this aspect of the clinic's operations.

▌Application Exercise

To secure a loan from the bank, Taylor must present a detailed business plan. Prepare such a plan as if you were in Taylor's position. Be sure to include the following elements:

- A statement of the activities the clinic will engage in
- A market analysis detailing the clinic's competitive advantages, an analysis of the competition, pricing structure, and a marketing plan
- The credentials of the clinic's principal owners and operators
- Historical and projected cash flow and income statements
- A breakdown of costs associated with the project based on the schematics developed by the architect
- The amount of personal equity committed by the athletic trainer
- The amount of the loan being requested

▌ For background information on concepts presented in Case Study 7, see *Management Strategies in Athletic Training*, chapters 2, 4, and 5.

CASE STUDY 8

∎ **Topic:**   Designing a college sports medicine facility

∎ **Setting:**   College

∎ **Primary concept:**   Facility planning

∎ **Secondary concepts:**   Program planning and evaluation
Communication

Holly Dolan was excited about getting started on the task before her. After finding out yesterday that the college was finally going to build a new training room, she had immediately focused on the facility design she would submit to the planning committee. The new training room was just one part of a much larger project to construct a general campus recreation and athletic facility. The largest portion of the money for the new building had come from the Brookhouse Foundation, and the building was to be named the Brookhouse Health and Physical Education Center. In addition to the new training room, the building would house the offices of the Physical Education and Athletics Department, weight room, three-court gymnasium, running track, dance studio, swimming pool, class-rooms, locker rooms, and an exercise physiology lab. It would also include an area of "dead" space, the purpose of which had not yet been specified.

Holly had always had a vision for the college's sports medicine program that included bringing all of the campus's health-related resources into one location. She felt that by bringing health services together the college would be more likely to achieve its goal of developing a model of holistic wellness for all its students. Unfortunately, she wasn't sure how the health service director would feel about relocating the college health clinic from the small house it now occupied on the edge of campus. Similarly, she worried that the director of the counseling center might balk at the idea as well.

Holly decided that the best approach would be to draw some preliminary plans that incorporated the training room, health clinic, counseling center, and exercise physiology lab into a unified operation in its own corner of the building (see Figure 1). After she discussed the plan with the architect, she forwarded a copy to the planning committee and to the directors of the health service and the counseling center. Unfortunately, neither the health service director nor the counseling center director was enthusiastic about the idea. Both were content to run their programs in isolation as they had been doing for years. Holly was upset at their inflexibility. She was sure that her ideas would result in better services for all the college's students, not just her athletes.

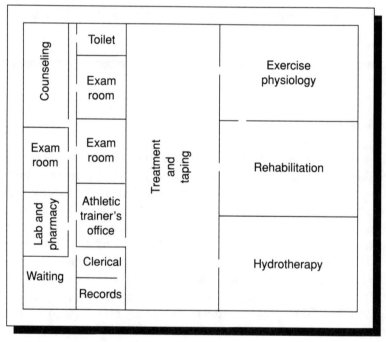

▮ Figure 1   Holly's drawing of the proposed wellness center.

▮ Analysis Questions

1. What are the strengths of Holly's proposal? What are the weaknesses?

2. If you were in Holly's position, would you recommend a similar design? Why or why not? What changes would you recommend?

3. What other alternatives exist for developing the holistic health model that Holly desires?

4. If you were in Holly's position, would you have followed a similar course of action to try to build support for your ideas? Why or why not? If not, what would you do differently?

5. What actions could Holly take to see her plan implemented? What allies might she enlist? What are the risks, if any, of pursuing this plan against the wishes of the health service and counseling center directors?

▌ Application Exercises

1. Design your own training room to support the activities of a college or university sports medicine program. Consider the following facts:
   - 500 student-athletes
   - 18 intercollegiate sports, including football
   - 2 full-time and one graduate assistant athletic trainers
   - $50,000 budget for new equipment and furniture

2. Describe the steps you used to develop your design. Include your rationale for each design element, including square footage, special function area layout, systems specifications, and equipment purchases and placement.

▌ For background information on concepts presented in Case Study 8, see *Management Strategies in Athletic Training*, chapters 2, 4, and 5.

CASE STUDY 9

Topic: Planning for emergencies

Setting: High school

Primary concept: Policy and procedure development

Secondary concepts: Program planning and evaluation
Legal liability
Financial management

The day had gone surprisingly well considering all the activity at Central High School. Central was both hosting the league track championships and playing a baseball doubleheader against the crosstown rivals. Martha Cunningham, Central's athletic trainer, was attempting to cover both events with a staff of two student athletic trainers. She was hopeful that her team physician would show up at some point, although he wasn't sure if he could make it. Martha decided to place one student trainer at the baseball game and the other at the track meet while she walked back and forth between the events. Fortunately, the baseball field was directly adjacent to the track, so Martha was confident she could keep a close eye on both events.

During the boys 5,000-meter run, several of the girls were warming up for their 3,000-meter race, which would follow immediately. Martha was concerned about one of the boys, who looked like he was having a problem with his hamstring. He started the race with an elastic bandage wrapped around his thigh, but he had stopped midway through the race to remove it. Now he was limping noticeably. Finally, Martha saw him fall to the track in pain and frustration.

Martha told Todd, the student trainer covering the track meet, that she would run over and take care of the injured boy. When she got there, however, she found two injured athletes—as Martha was jogging over to attend to the injured boy, a girl who was warming up for the 3,000-meter race was hit in the side of the head with a foul ball from the baseball game. It was immediately evident that the girl was injured more seriously than the boy, although he was exhibiting considerable discomfort. Martha performed a quick examination of the girl's closed head injury and decided that she would require additional medical evaluation as soon as possible. Because the girl was not fully conscious, Martha decided to summon an ambulance to make the transfer to the hospital.

While Martha immobilized the girl's cervical spine, she told one of the Central athletes who had gathered around to go find Todd to tell him to call the ambulance. The athlete ran off, but returned several minutes later and informed Martha that he couldn't find Todd among the hundreds of athletes and spectators present for the meet. Martha then instructed the athlete to make the call himself. She told him that the telephone was located in the custodian's office just inside the school's back door. Twenty minutes later the ambulance finally arrived and took the girl to the hospital. One of Central's booster club officers accompanied the girl in the ambulance because her parents had not been able to attend the meet and her coach was the only adult who could stay to supervise the other squad members. After the ambulance left, Martha turned her attention to the boy with the hamstring problem, but he was nowhere to be found. He had apparently wandered away after it became clear that nobody was going to pay attention to his injury.

When Martha found the athlete she had sent to make the phone call, she asked why it had taken so long for the ambulance to arrive. He informed her that the custodian's office was locked and that it had taken him about 10 min to find someone with a key. After the track meet and the baseball game ended, Martha went to the hospital to visit the injured girl. The doctor informed her that the girl would be fine and was due to be released shortly.

Three weeks later Martha received a phone call from the injured girl's track coach. He wanted to know if Central High was going to pay the ambulance and hospital bills. His reasoning was that because the accident happened at Central High School, a Central staff member directed that the ambulance be called, and the girl's parents were uninsured, Central should pay the bills. Martha was very surprised when the coach said that someone on Central's staff had told the girl that Central had insurance for this kind of situation and not to worry about the bills. Martha told him that she thought his school would be responsible but that his athletic director should call her athletic director to discuss the matter.

▌ Analysis Questions

1. How would the presence of a comprehensive emergency plan have helped Martha handle this situation with greater effectiveness and efficiency?
2. What elements would you include in an emergency plan if you were in Martha's position?
3. Is the injured girl's track coach justified in his request that Central High School pay for the ambulance and hospital bills? Why or why not? If not, who do you think should be responsible? What procedures should be followed to determine who will pay the bills?
4. Is this the kind of injury that most athletic insurance policies would cover?

▌ Application Exercise

Devise an emergency plan for your school. Be sure to include all the elements you mentioned in your answer to question 2. Check your school's policy to see if this injury would be covered under the terms of the policy.

▌ For background information on concepts presented in Case Study 9, see *Management Strategies in Athletic Training*, chapters 2, 4, 7, and 8.

CASE STUDY 10

■ **Topic:** Developing a drug and alcohol policy

■ **Setting:** College

■ **Primary concept:** Policy and procedure development

■ **Secondary concept:** Program planning and evaluation

When Jon Jackson picked up the newspaper on his way to work, he wasn't surprised to see a story detailing the police breakup of another post–football game party that had turned violent. Since Jon's appointment as head athletic trainer at State University 5 years before, he had seen the problems related to the use of alcohol and other drugs become increasingly worse. His athletes were frequently involved in legal and university judicial actions stemming from the drinking that seemed to be rampant on campus.

Jon arrived at the fieldhouse to find a note on the training room door asking him to report to the AD's office as soon as possible. He went there immediately and was met by a distressed Quentin Carmichael, State University's athletic director for the past 25 years. "Jon," he began, "I've got a problem. We've got a problem. The president of the university called me last night and really jumped down my throat about this alcohol situation. Have you heard about last night's party? It was the straw that broke the camel's back, and he's telling me that if we don't get the problem under control, he'll get somebody in here who can. Needless to say, I thought of you immediately, Jon. You're our medical man. I'm counting on you to be our point man for this. The first thing I want you to do is come up with a policy that specifically addresses the drug and alcohol problem. After we get that in place we'll sit down and see what

else needs to get done to curb this thing. Get to work, Jon. I want that
policy in place soon.''

Jon had mixed feelings about the meeting. He didn't mind becoming
involved with trying to help stem the alcohol problem, but he sensed that
the AD was throwing the entire problem in his lap. He was certain he
wouldn't be able to change things by himself.

Later that day, Jon began to write the policy Carmichael had requested.
He worked late into the evening. The next morning he delivered the
following document to Quentin Carmichael:

State University Athletic Department
Policy on Alcohol, Tobacco, and Other Drug Use

Statement of Problem

The State University Athletic Department recognizes the use of alcohol, tobacco, and other drugs as a significant problem for many student-athletes that results in negative effects on behavior, relationships, academic performance, and the overall learning environment. The use and misuse of these substances also affects athletic performance as well as team and university morale.

Statement of Purpose

The State University Athletic Department Policy on Alcohol, Tobacco, and Other Drug Use is designed to meet the following objectives:

1. *Protect the health and safety of student-athletes*
2. *Promote fair competition*
3. *Help students make responsible decisions about the use of alcohol, tobacco, and other drugs*
4. *Help students who desire to resist pressure to use any substance*
5. *Promote a sense of order and discipline*
6. *Promote team unity*
7. *Help students who may be in need of health or counseling services*

Statement of Rules

All State University student-athletes shall adhere to all university policies with regard to alcohol and other drug use. In addition, during the season of competition and when representing the university or team, a student-athlete shall not use, regardless of quantity, be in possession of, or distribute any (a) beverage containing alcohol, (b) form of tobacco, (c) other illegal drugs. In addition, the student-athlete shall not use anabolic-androgenic steroids or any other drug prohibited by the NCAA throughout the entire year. It is not a violation for a student-athlete to be in possession of or use a drug prescribed for the student-athlete's use by her/his physician if consistent with NCAA policy and regulations. A violation is deemed to have occurred if a coach becomes aware, from any source, of any instance in which the statement of rules has been breached. In cases where a student-athlete disputes the facts presented by the coach, an appeal may be made to a committee comprised of two athletic directors, the head athletic trainer, and one male and one female team captain to be elected by all team captains. The decision of the Appeals Committee will be final.

Statement of Consequences

These are the consequences for violating this rule:

1. **First violation**: After confirmation of the first violation, the student-athlete shall meet with the coach and athletic director and then discuss the violation with team members at a team meeting. The student will be referred to the Student Development Office if a violation of university policy is involved.
2. **Second violation**: After confirmation of the second violation, the student-athlete shall lose eligibility for 1 week or two playing dates, whichever is less. The student-athlete shall continue to practice with the team and be in attendance at any games, but shall not dress for the game. The student-athlete shall also be referred to the Student Development Office.
3. **Third violation**: After confirmation of the third violation, the student-athlete shall be suspended for the remainder of the academic year. The student-athlete shall also be referred to the Student Development Office.
4. Consequences shall be accumulative across seasons, beginning with and throughout the student-athlete's participation on a State University athletic team.

Statement of Education and Prevention

The State University Athletic Department recognizes its role in preventing alcohol, tobacco, and other drug use by student-athletes and promoting health as part of this policy. The Athletic Department will regularly provide the following educational opportunities:

1. *Safe, ethical, and healthy training programs that are not enhanced by drugs for staff and student-athletes*
2. *In-service training for coaches and other athletic department staff*
3. *Print material on alcohol, tobacco, and other drugs for student athletes, coaches, parents, and other athletic staff*
4. *Opportunities for coaches, student-athletes, and other athletic staff to discuss alcohol, tobacco, and other drug use issues and problems.*

Statement of Policy Review

This policy shall be reviewed and revised or affirmed annually by the Appeals Committee. The Appeals Committee will forward its recommendations to the State University Athletic Department for final approval.

Jon's policy was met with great enthusiasm by Quentin Carmichael. "I'm going to make sure this is sent to every athlete in the program," he exclaimed. "We'll show the president that we can deal seriously with this problem. Good work, Jon!"

▌ Analysis Questions

1. What criticisms, if any, do you have regarding the process used to develop and implement this policy? Would you have done anything differently? If so, what and why?

2. Does the "policy" that Jon drafted meet all the criteria and accomplish the purposes that a policy is supposed to?

3. What are the strengths of the policy? What are the weaknesses? What elements of the policy would you change? How would you change them? Why?

4. How effective is this policy likely to be in changing the attitudes and behaviors of State University student-athletes? Justify your answer.

■ Application Exercise

Using Jon's "policy" as a general statement of principles, design an educational program to help combat the inappropriate use of alcohol and other drugs by college-aged student-athletes. Be sure to include time lines, descriptions of materials, learning objectives, and evaluation methods.

■ For background information on concepts presented in Case Study 10, see *Management Strategies in Athletic Training*, chapter 2.

CASE STUDY 11

▮ Topic: Developing the athletic medicine model in industrial settings

▮ Setting: Industrial

▮ Primary concept: Program planning and evaluation

▮ Secondary concepts: Human resources
Communication
Ethics

Alice Epstein was more than a little nervous. Although her interviews with the director of human resources and the plant manager had gone well, she knew that if she didn't impress the CEO of Titan Industries she wouldn't get the job she wanted so desperately. Alice had discovered this job opportunity a month ago when a fellow athletic trainer who was employed in an industrial setting on the opposite side of town called and told her that his boss had convinced the people at Titan to give the athletic trainer health care model a try. Alice had submitted her credentials to the human resources office and received a phone call the next week asking her to come for an interview.

Alice was ushered into the CEO's office. "Good morning, Alice, I'm Harvey Oldham," said the CEO. "Thanks for coming today. I hope you enjoyed your tour of our manufacturing plant. Alice, let me come right to the point. Our medical costs are running out of control. It's the single largest cost we have. We spend more on medical care for our employees than we do on steel for our products. It has to stop if we are going to remain competitive. I've been talking to some of my colleagues in industry and they have great things to say about how they are using athletic trainers to aggressively treat injured workers right in the plant. I like the idea. I want to hire you to run this operation for me here at Titan. Our human resources director thinks you're top drawer, and his judgment has always been sound. You've already been told about the salary and benefits. Do you want the job?'' ''Absolutely!'' replied Alice. ''Good,'' responded Oldham. ''I have to warn you about one thing, however. We begin negotiations for a new contract with the union in 2 weeks. You are part of my management team. I want that fully understood. This in-house rehabilitation program may be a cause for concern among some members of the union. They may see it as an infringement on their right to choose their own health care providers. They may see it as a company attempt to keep injured workers on the job. They may see it as a lot of things that you and I don't intend it to be. I don't want this to become a major issue. To see that it doesn't, I want a proposal for your program's operations by next week. In addition, be prepared to spend at least one day explaining it to the union's negotiating team if it comes up during the bargaining sessions. Welcome to the Titan family!''

When Alice left Harvey Oldham's office her head was spinning. Not only had she just entered the world of gainful employment, she was overwhelmed by the enormity of her responsibilities. She knew she had plenty of work ahead of her, so she decided to get started immediately.

▮ Analysis Questions

1. If you were in Alice's position, what questions would you need answered prior to developing the program proposal? What process would you follow to get the information you needed?

2. What arguments would you use when attempting to persuade the union that the in-house injury prevention and treatment program would be a benefit for its members? What evidence would you offer in support of your arguments? What allies could you enlist in this effort that the union would view as credible?

3. What problems will Alice likely encounter because of her dual role as an agent of management and a health care professional who the injured workers of Titan Industries are supposed to be able to trust? What strategies should Alice consider to avoid these problems?

▌ Application Exercise

Write an industrial in-house injury prevention and treatment program proposal. Assume that the company for which you are writing the proposal is a manufacturer of power tools for the retail hardware market. Assume the plant employs 500 workers in three shifts and is located in a midsized city with a hospital and a full range of medical specialists. Further assume that there are two outpatient physical therapy clinics in the community.

▌ For background information on concepts presented in Case Study 11, see *Management Strategies in Athletic Training*, chapters 1, 2, 3, and 5.

CASE STUDY 12

■ **Topic:** Managing sensitive information

■ **Setting:** High school

■ **Primary concept:** Information management

■ **Secondary concepts:** Policy and procedure development
Legal liability
Ethics

Mindy Jackson had been an athletic trainer and health teacher at Kennedy High School for 10 years. During that time, she had come to be a trusted and respected member of the school staff. The coaching staff loved her. The students thought she was great because she always seemed to have time to listen to their problems. The parents' club had even made her an honorary alumnus in a ceremony during halftime of one of the basketball games last year.

Mindy was growing increasingly concerned about Sally Jones, one of her favorite kids on the volleyball team. Sally and her parents had been an important part of Mindy's life for several years. They were neighbors. Sally's mother, Jean Jones, was one of Mindy's closest friends, and Sally was the regular babysitter for Mindy's two young children. Sally was usually one of the most happy-go-lucky kids in the school. The past 2 weeks, however, she had seemed sullen and withdrawn. At first, Mindy thought that Sally might just be tired from the long volleyball season that was coming to an end. She thought her changed attitude also could have something to do with Sally's relationship with her boyfriend, which was on shaky ground according to the high school rumor mill.

One day after practice Sally asked Mindy if she could have a ride home. Mindy was just locking up anyway so she readily agreed. During the ride home, Mindy was once again reminded of the change in Sally's personality. Finally, she decided to try to find out what was bothering her. When Mindy asked why she had been so forlorn lately, Sally burst into tears and buried her head in her hands. Mindy pulled over and allowed Sally to collect herself. "Sally, what's wrong?" Mindy asked softly. "Promise me you won't tell anybody about this," sobbed Sally. "Of course I won't," replied Mindy. "I'm so glad to finally have somebody to talk to," cried Sally. "These last 2 weeks have been hell and there just hasn't been anybody I can turn to. About a month ago Jeff and I went to a party. Jeff was drinking a lot. Later we drove around for awhile and ended up parking and, well, Jeff forced himself on me. I told him I didn't want to—that I wasn't ready—but he wouldn't stop. Now I'm almost sure I'm pregnant. I'm 2 weeks overdue. I'm so scared, Mindy!"

Mindy's immediate concern was Sally's health status. She agreed to help her purchase a home pregnancy test, which revealed that Sally was, in fact, pregnant. Unfortunately, Mindy knew that her toughest decisions were yet to come.

▌ Analysis Questions

1. Who, if anyone, should Mindy confide in regarding Sally's pregnancy? How much, if anything, should she tell them about the circumstances of the situation? Does Sally's volleyball coach have a need to know? Do her parents?

2. What referral process would you follow if you were in Mindy's position? What alternatives exist? What are the strengths and weaknesses of each?

3. What are Mindy's legal responsibilities in this case? How are they likely to conflict with her personal relationship with Sally? With Sally's parents? With the school community?

▌ Application Exercise

Design a release of medical information form that could be signed by athletes and would indicate their consent for release of medical information. Write a policy statement and supporting procedures that address the confidentiality of patient medical records.

▌ For background information on concepts presented in Case Study 12, see *Management Strategies in Athletic Training*, chapters 2, 6, and 8.

CASE STUDY 13

■ **Topic:** Employee classification

■ **Setting:** College

■ **Primary concept:** Human resources

■ **Secondary concept:** Legal liability

Wendy Trenton received the following memo in her campus mailbox:

To: All Athletic Department Administrators

From: Edward Bell, Athletic Director

Subject: State Employee Commission

Please note that a representative of the State Employee Commission will be here on Monday. As most of you know, the commission is the arm of the state government charged with oversight of all agencies that employ persons on the state payroll. The commission conducts an audit of state institutions every 5 years. The commission's representative will spend approximately 15 minutes with each of you. My secretary will be in touch to inform you of your appointment time.

When Wendy arrived for her appointment on Monday, she was introduced to the commission's representative, Stan Altman. "Sorry for this imposition on your time," he began. "I just have a few questions and then I'll let you go. The first thing I need to make sure of is that your job classification is correct. My notes indicate that you are the head athletic trainer here at the university. Is that correct?" "That's right," replied Wendy.

"Good," said Stan. "Now, I also see that you are classified as an administrator. Tell me, Wendy, do you have the authority to hire and fire employees?" "Well, not exactly," replied Wendy. "I conduct the search and make a recommendation to the athletic director. He definitely has the last word on who gets hired and fired." "I see," Stan muttered suspiciously. "Well," he continued, "you certainly must have control over your own budget." "Not exactly," stammered Wendy. "I submit a budget request to the AD every year. He always modifies it and lets me know what the final figure is. When I submit purchase orders for goods and services, the business office won't process them unless Ed Bell has signed them." Stan finished the interview with a few more questions and told Wendy that if he needed to talk to her again he would call.

Two weeks later Wendy received the following letter:

Dear Ms. Trenton:

Thank you for agreeing to meet with me a couple of weeks ago. After carefully reviewing the record of our interview and conducting other detailed checks of your state employment files, the State Employee Commission has ruled that you have been inappropriately categorized as an administrator during your 10-year tenure at the university. In fact, you should have been categorized as nonexempt staff when you were originally hired. Your employment status has been officially altered to reflect this finding.

As a nonexempt staff member, you must limit the number of hours you work during any 7-day period to no more than 40. Should you work more than 40 hours in any week, you are entitled to overtime pay at 1.5 times your calculated hourly wage rate. Although your work has greatly exceeded this limit during each of the past 10 years, you are eligible to receive back-pay for your overtime hours for no more than the past 3 years.

Sincerely,

Stanley Altman
State Employee Commission

cc: Edward Bell

Wendy read the letter three times before rushing up to Ed Bell's office. When she arrived it was clear that Ed had already received and read his copy of the letter and was not pleased about it. Ed explained to Wendy that the State Employee Commission expected the athletic department to come up with the back-pay mentioned in the letter. Wendy told him that in order to meet the 40-hour rule, the department would have to add at least two additional athletic trainers. "I'll be damned if we're going to add staff or start paying overtime around here," announced Ed defiantly. "I think I should call my lawyer," Wendy shot back as she stormed out of Ed's office.

■ Analysis Questions

1. What alternative actions could Wendy take in light of the commission's ruling? What are the strengths and weaknesses of each of these alternatives?

2. Wendy has implied that she may pursue legal action against the athletic department to ensure that she receives her back-pay and additional staff. Is this the proper course of action? Why or why not?

3. What risks does Wendy face by pursuing legal action? What are the possible benefits? Do the possible benefits outweigh the risks?

4. What allies could Wendy enlist to help her pursue her rights under the commission's ruling? How should they be used?

5. What alternatives does Ed Bell have? Which would be the least costly? Which is most likely to preserve a positive working relationship with Wendy?

■ Application Exercise

Develop a position description for Wendy. Be sure to delineate the following:

- The qualifications Wendy should have to hold the position
- The responsibilities for which Wendy will be held accountable
- The relative importance of Wendy's responsibilities
- The timetable for review and revision of the position description

---

■ For background information on concepts presented in Case Study 13, see *Management Strategies in Athletic Training*, chapter 3.

CASE STUDY 14

▮ Topic: Conflict management

▮ Setting: High school/Clinical

▮ Primary concept: Human resources

▮ Secondary concept: Communication

Katrina Tabman was well liked by most of the staff at Northwestern High School, where she was an athletic trainer contracted to the school by her employer, the Wellness Center. The center was a physician-owned rehabilitation and fitness facility with contracts to provide sports medicine services at seven local high schools. Katrina worked in the clinic in the morning and then went over to the school around 2:00. Because she spent so much time at the school, most of the coaches had come to think of her as one of the regular employees of the school system. Everyone but Jock Barnes, that is. Jock had been the school's varsity football coach for the past 30 years. He had seven state championship trophies in his office. He was a legend.

The problems between Katrina and Jock had started almost as soon as Katrina arrived 2 years ago. Because the school had never employed an athletic trainer before, Jock was used to handling all his players' medical concerns. When Katrina started providing Jock with daily written reports on the health and practice status of his players, Jock told her that he had been in the business long enough to know when a kid could play and when he couldn't. When Katrina suggested that Jock needn't tape certain kids in the locker room prior to practices and games anymore, he told her to start paying more attention to the volleyball and field hockey teams and less to his boys. In short, Katrina and Jock just didn't get along.

One Monday morning after Katrina and Jock had had another argument following a Friday night game, Randy Jensen, the director of athletic training outreach services at the Wellness Center, called Katrina into his office. Randy explained that Jock had called one of the physician-owners of the center and threatened to use his influence to see that the school pulled out of the contract unless a new athletic trainer was assigned to Northwestern High. Not only would he see to it that the school backed out of the contract, but he also would send all his players in need of orthopedic services to another group on the other side of town. Randy told Katrina that the doctor had defended her as a loyal and competent professional. After a long conversation, he apparently was successful in getting Jock to back down from his threat. Both the physician and Randy did want Katrina to know, however, that this situation was becoming a problem that they didn't need. Randy told Katrina that he expected her to "play it cool" with Jock and do everything in her power to avoid further conflicts. If things didn't improve, they might have to reassign Katrina to another school next fall.

Katrina was upset and angry after the meeting with Randy. Although she was glad that the physician-owner had defended her, she felt that undue pressure was being put on her to resolve the conflict. She wasn't sure how she could do it in light of her feeling that Jock would never change. Except for Jock, she really liked working at Northwestern High. She didn't want to leave, but she didn't want to violate her own principles or standards either.

▌ Analysis Questions

1. What role could Randy play to facilitate a resolution to this conflict? What alternatives are available to him? What actions would you take if you were in his position? Why?

2. What are the risks associated with leaving Katrina assigned to Northwestern High School? What are the benefits? For the Wellness Center? For Katrina? If you were in Randy's position, would you reassign Katrina? Why or why not?

3. What strategies, if any, would you employ to ease tensions if you were in Katrina's position? What are the risks and benefits of each of these strategies?

4. What allies could Katrina employ to support her position? Are they likely to be helpful in this case? Why or why not?

▌ Application Exercise

Assume that Katrina was reassigned to another school for the next fall and that you have been assigned to replace her at Northwestern High. What strategies would you use to avoid the conflict that existed when she worked there?

▌ For background information on concepts presented in Case Study 14, see *Management Strategies in Athletic Training*, chapters 1 and 2.

CASE STUDY 15

■ **Topic:** Developing programs in a hospital setting

■ **Setting:** Clinical

■ **Primary concept:** Program planning and evaluation

■ **Secondary concepts:** Human resources
Policy and procedure development
Communication
Financial management

When Carlton Albers, PT, was hired to direct the rehabilitation services department at Memorial Hospital he was given a very specific mandate from the vice president for clinical services: Reorganize the department to improve efficiency. The VP was convinced that the department didn't generate nearly the revenue it could simply because its people weren't utilized properly. Although rehabilitation services was the leading revenue-producing department in terms of outpatient dollar production the VP was convinced it could do better, and he communicated this to Carlton in very strong terms.

When Carlton arrived the department was staffed by six full-time physical therapists, three PT aids, one occupational therapist, one speech therapist, and one full-time and three part-time certified athletic trainers (ATCs). Most patients were either inpatients or outpatients referred from the one orthopedic group in town. Occasionally a patient would be referred from one of the family practitioners, but this was rare. Policies and procedures, where they existed at all, were lax. There was no policy and procedures manual. Patient charting was performed longhand on legal-sized sheets of white paper with the hospital letterhead stamped at the top. The athletic trainers were used like aides, performing various therapeutic procedures under the direction of the physical therapists.

Carlton called a meeting of the department staff at noon on his first day at Memorial. "Thanks for giving up part of your lunch hour," he began. "Folks, when I was hired to run this department I was given a very specific charge—to tighten things up around here and make us more efficient. Although I intend to do just that, I want to get to know each of you a little better. In about 2 weeks we'll meet again and I'll let you know what changes are coming. In the meantime, I want you to carry on just as you have been so I can get a better feel for how the department has operated in the past." The meeting broke up with confusion among the staff. Carlton went back to his office and immediately began drafting a new set of policies and procedures for the department.

As he promised, Carlton called a meeting 2 weeks later at which he passed out the new policies and procedures manual. The manual covered everything from patient charting and treatment protocols to lunch breaks and sick leave. Every vestige of how the department operated in the past was gone and replaced with something new. The biggest change came in how department personnel were to be used. Carlton had received permission to bring the three part-time ATCs on as full-time staff. From now on, each PT would be teamed with an ATC as an equal partner in the treatment process for every patient. The aides would be used as "swing" personnel to fill in when needed and for many of the more routine and technical tasks. The two PTs not specifically teamed with an ATC would be used to develop rehabilitation service contracts with two large companies in town. Each PT/ATC team would be responsible for developing a contractual relationship with a high school athletic program in one of the area schools. The occupational and speech therapists were given caseload quotas far exceeding their previous loads. The organizational chart for the newly organized program is shown in Figure 2.

■ Analysis Questions

1. How is Carlton's agenda for change likely to be received by the various members of the department? Why?

2. Analyze the process Carlton used to reorganize the department. Was it sound? What, if anything, would you have done differently given the same mandate from the vice president?

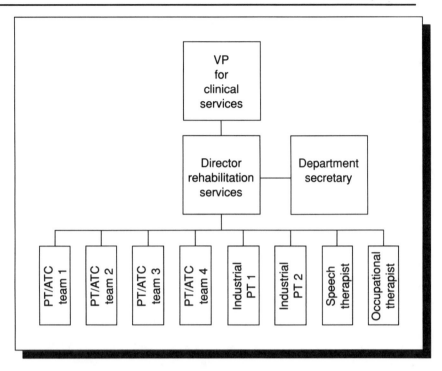

I Figure 2   Carlton's new organizational structure.

3. How successful is the new deployment of personnel likely to be? Why? Is this the way you would have deployed the department's personnel? If not, how would you have done it?

4. What are the strengths and weaknesses of the PT/ATC team concept?

5. Is Carlton's outreach approach to industry and high school sports medicine programs likely to generate significant revenues? Why or why not? What circumstances must be present for these programs to be financially successful? How can the department bring about these circumstances?

6. What are the strengths and weaknesses of Carlton's new organizational structure? What suggestions, if any, do you have for its improvement?

I Application Exercise

Take part in a role-playing exercise in which you play the part of Carlton Albers and two other students or colleagues act as members of a PT/ATC team. Pretend that you are interviewing them in order to determine their perceptions about how the department should be organized. Afterward, develop your organizational scheme for the department. Allow the members of the PT/ATC team to read and reflect on your plan. Interview them again to see how they feel about the plan.

_____

▌ For background information on concepts presented in Case Study 15, see *Management Strategies in Athletic Training*, chapters 1, 2, and 3.

■ **Topic:** Avoiding legal liability

■ **Setting:** Industrial

■ **Primary concept:** Legal liability

■ **Secondary concepts:** Communication
Information management

When Tad Raymond, ATC, looked up from the work he was doing at his desk, he was surprised to see two men entering the industrial sports medicine clinic he directed at Giant Industries. "Are you Tad Raymond?" the uniformed policeman asked. Tad nodded yes. "I'm deputy sheriff Bart Creel and I have a court order requiring you to appear before Judge Byron Haskell on charges of violating the medical practice act of our state." The deputy handed the summons to Tad, who looked like he might fall over at any minute. "Tad Raymond," the other man said, "This is a copy of a civil lawsuit charging you with negligence in the treatment of injuries suffered by Mr. Clyde Cantrell. My name is Rusty Lawson and I am Mr. Cantrell's legal counsel. Better have your attorney give me a buzz, Mr. Raymond." The two men turned and walked out.

After Tad composed himself he picked up the phone and dialed his uncle, who practiced law in the next county. Tad explained what had just transpired and his uncle agreed to meet him later that day to discuss the case. "Don't talk to anyone about this," warned the uncle. "Chances are, the company and the doctor are being sued too. They're dragging you into this to see if they can't use you to get to the serious money. I'll review the state medical practice act this afternoon and let you know what I come up with when I see you later."

When Tad met his uncle later that day, he explained his side of the story. Clyde Cantrell was a 55-year-old worker at Giant Industries who had operated a pedal-activated drill press for 20 years. A few months ago Cantrell had been playing softball on one of the company fields during his lunch break when he stepped in a hole and twisted his ankle. A few of his buddies brought him into Tad's clinic where Tad evaluated the injury, wrapped ice on the ankle, fit him with crutches, and called Cantrell's wife to take him to the hospital for X rays. When Cantrell came into Tad's clinic the next morning, he told Tad that the emergency room doctor said the injury was just a sprain and that he would probably need to stay off it for a couple of weeks. The company physician who acted as medical director for Tad's industrial sports medicine program was coming later that morning, so Tad decided to pull Cantrell off the line and treat him in the clinic until the doctor arrived and could look at the injury. Cantrell said that was fine by him.

When the doctor arrived and evaluated the injury, he told Tad that Cantrell had a second-degree ankle sprain and to treat it "as necessary." Cantrell could perform other kinds of jobs that didn't require the use of his feet until the injury healed. Cantrell thought that was a good idea. He was placed in another job where he could sit down. Tad pulled him off the line twice a day to treat his ankle in the clinic. After about 3 weeks, Cantrell's ankle looked normal, but he still limped and complained about the pain whenever Tad asked him when he would be ready to return to his old job. After 2 months, Cantrell's foreman came to Tad and asked what was taking so long. Tad told him he thought Cantrell's ankle was basically fine. The foreman ordered Cantrell back to the drill press. Cantrell told the foreman he wasn't ready yet. The foreman fired Cantrell.

When Tad finished telling the story, his uncle smiled and told him he shouldn't have much to worry about. "I checked the state medical practice act," he said. "Even though there isn't any licensure for athletic trainers in our state, it clearly says that physicians can delegate certain functions and procedures. As long as you have the paperwork that proves the doctor ordered the procedures and was actively involved in supervision of the case, I *think* you'll be OK. The negligence charge could be a little more difficult to avoid. They'll have to meet a number of legal tests, though. If your records can demonstrate that your treatment met the standard of care, you should be OK there too."

▌ Analysis Questions

1. Could Tad have done anything to avoid the legal problem he now faces?
2. How can Tad safeguard his personal financial resources in the face of such charges?
3. Is there anything about the working relationship between Tad and the company physician that would give cause for concern in this case?
4. What kinds of records should Tad be able to produce to defend himself against these charges?
5. If Tad eventually has to go to court to defend himself against either of these charges, what kinds of expert witnesses might he enlist to strengthen his case?
6. What legal tests will Cantrell have to prove to support his charge of negligence?
7. To what standard of care is Tad likely to be held? Why?

▌ Application Exercise

What are the legal limits of an athletic trainer's practice in your state? From what statutes are these limits derived? How might they be applied in an industrial setting? Check with your state athletic trainers association to find out where to find the appropriate statutes.

▌ For background information on concepts presented in Case Study 16, see *Management Strategies in Athletic Training*, chapters 6 and 8.

CASE STUDY 17

■ **Topic:** Capital improvements

■ **Setting:** College

■ **Primary concept:** Financial management

■ **Secondary concept:** Program planning and evaluation

The bad news was that Mary Wolters's budget was just about busted—again—and the winter sports season hadn't even ended. Mary had always operated the City Junior College sports medicine program on a budget that most athletic trainers would find impossibly meager. She took a certain pride that she was able to stretch her resources as far as she did. One problem she wasn't sure how to solve, creatively or otherwise, was what to do about her aging equipment. Her modalities broke down so often she was seriously considering not having them repaired. She requested the funds to purchase new equipment every year, but every year she was turned down. It was depressing.

The good news was that the chairperson of the physical education department had just informed her of a wonderful opportunity that might remedy the situation. An old college buddy of his was now director of research and development at Mackenzie Medical Co. Mackenzie had just developed a new analgesic cream designed to relieve muscular aches and pains, and the company needed to test the product for efficacy prior to obtaining FDA approval. The director had asked if anyone at City Junior College could run the clinical trials for the cream, and the chairperson had immediately thought of Mary. Mackenzie would pay her $1,000 and the college $25,000 to conduct the trials. Mackenzie would provide all the materials, design the research protocol, and analyze the data. The only thing Mary would have to do is find 150 subjects over a 9-month period and implement the test protocols with each of them. The chairperson was willing to let Mary use the $25,000 for her program in any way she wanted.

Although Mary had several concerns, she immediately accepted the offer. She was very excited about the prospect of a $25,000 infusion into her program. She wasn't sure where she was going to find the time to conduct the work the study required, however. Between her athletic training duties and her teaching, she already carried one of the heaviest loads in the department. The study would require a 30-min interview with each subject both before and after the clinical trial. That amounted to 150 hours she was going to have to find somewhere. "Oh well," thought Mary, "creativity is my middle name!"

▌Analysis Questions

1. What alternatives should Mary consider for using the $25,000 given her small budget and the poor state of her equipment? What options does she have?
2. Which of the options you developed would you choose? Why? What are the disadvantages, if any, of choosing this option?
3. How can Mary best manage her time during the course of the clinical trials to both handle her normal work load and complete the clinical trials?
4. According to the case description, Mary made the decision to undertake the project "immediately." What are the risks of jumping to such a quick decision? What are the risks associated with postponing the decision? What strategies might Mary have used to give herself more time to critically examine the proposal?

▌Application Exercise

Develop an inventory of the durable equipment at your institution. Develop a maintenance schedule for each piece of equipment. Develop a depreciation schedule and a plan to replace each piece. Be sure to provide a budget for maintenance, depreciation, and equipment replacement.

▌For background information on concepts presented in Case Study 17, see *Management Strategies in Athletic Training*, chapters 2 and 4.

CASE STUDY 18

■ **Topic:** Records automation

■ **Setting:** College

■ **Primary concept:** Information management

■ **Secondary concept:** Policy and procedure development

"Robert," the AD said as he poured coffee after lunch, "all of us here at the Great Plains University Athletic Department hope you'll be willing to take the position of head athletic trainer that I'm offering you. We think you're the best man for the job. You'd be filling big shoes, of course. Lump Doherty was a giant in your field and here at GPU. His untimely death has left all of us in a state of shock, but we've got to move on. We'll always remember ol' Lump for his many good qualities, but between you and me, Lump was plain disorganized sometimes. His office down in the training room was easy to find once you waded through the paper. Heck, Lump bragged about the fact that he only saw the top of his desk once a year and that was when the janitor threatened to quit unless he cleaned the place up. Oh well, I shouldn't be trampling on his memory like this. Heck, I loved him. We all did."

Robert told the AD he would take the job. After he accepted the offer he flew home to prepare his family for the big move. Three weeks later they had purchased a house and moved in.

When Robert arrived for his first day as director of sports medicine at GPU, he couldn't believe the state of disarray that existed in his new office. The staff had decided to leave Lump's office just as it was and let Robert organize it as he saw fit. There was paper everywhere. Documents, files, records, reports, memos, and letters littered Robert's desk, even spilling onto the floor. Robert knew it would take some time to organize this aspect of the mess, but what really worried him were the six filing cabinets sitting in the corner. There seemed to be no rhyme or reason to how files were arranged. Budget information was mixed in with athletes' medical files. There were copies of letters dating back 20 years or more. Correspondence from the league and personnel folders were randomly stored with Lump's personal files and NATA information that dated back to the first conventions in the 1950s. There wasn't a computer in sight.

When Robert asked one of the assistants why everything was so disorganized, he was told that Lump insisted on handling all the filing himself. "He used to say that he was the one being paid to administer the program and so he should be the one to do this kind of work," the assistant continued. Robert scratched his head and called an immediate staff meeting to discuss the problem.

■ Analysis Questions

1. What are the disadvantages of having only one person on a staff of many solely responsible for information storage and retrieval? What are the advantages?

2. What advantages would be realized by computerizing the information management system at GPU? What aspects of the system are best suited for computerization?

3. If you were in Robert's position, how would you go about computerizing the information management system? What goals would you want to accomplish with the computerized system? What hardware and software would you select to help accomplish those goals? What policies, procedures, and practices should guide the new system?

■ Application Exercise

Robert will probably still have to store some information on paper. Develop a master outline for the filing system complete with major classifications and primary and secondary headings.

■ For background information on concepts presented in Case Study 18, see *Management Strategies in Athletic Training*, chapters 2 and 6.

CASE STUDY 19

■ **Topic:** Organizing physical examinations

■ **Setting:** High school

■ **Primary concept:** Policy and procedure development

■ **Secondary concepts:** Program planning and evaluation
Human resources
Communication
Legal liability

Steve Fu was the athletic trainer at John Kennedy High School. One of his responsibilities was to coordinate the annual physical examinations for all students planning to participate in interscholastic athletics. The school's policy was that every student-athlete must have a comprehensive physical examination administered by a licensed physician a maximum of 1 year prior to participation. When Dr. Martinson had been the school's team physician, he had conducted all the physicals at his office during two nights in the spring. If students failed to get a physical at that time, they had to get a physical from their own doctors. The new team physician, Dr. Mulligan, told Steve he wanted physicals administered differently. Instead of bringing the students to his office, he wanted to conduct the physicals in the gym. He told Steve to organize the details.

Steve decided to use a station approach. The girls would come the first night and the boys the second. Student-athletes would be evaluated at several stations, each run by a different volunteer. Steve figured he would need approximately 20 volunteers each night, at least four physicians, two nurses, and three athletic trainers or physical therapists from the local clinic along with coaches or parents. Steve decided to send out a letter to all of the medical and allied health volunteers. He asked the coach of each team to help and to bring one parent volunteer. He anticipated approximately 250 students each night.

When the first night of physicals finally arrived, Steve was surprised when nearly 300 students showed up. Unfortunately two of the physicians who had promised to come had been called to the hospital for emergencies. That left him with only two doctors for 300 physicals. After about the third hour of waiting in line, many of the students simply gave up and walked to the last station and turned in their physical cards without being examined by a doctor.

When the fall sports began practice in August, many of the coaches were furious that their best players couldn't begin practice because they hadn't had a physical examination. When Steve told the irate coaches that their athletes simply had to have a physical exam to participate, they decided to go over his head to the athletic director. The athletic director listened to their complaints and decided to allow those students without physicals to begin practicing as long as they received a physical before the first game. When Steve told Dr. Mulligan about the AD's decision, the team physician was so upset he decided to call his good friend, the school board president, to complain about the irrational and dangerous decision of the AD.

▌ Analysis Questions

1. What alternatives exist for organizing the physical exams? What are the strengths and weaknesses of each alternative?

2. Was Steve's method for organizing the physical exams effective? Was it efficient? How could it have been improved?

3. Was the high school's policy on physical examinations sound? Was it consistent with the physical examination policies of other athletic organizations (National Federation of State High School Associations [NFSHSA], NCAA, etc.)? Did the procedure established by Steve Fu adequately support the policy?

4. What are the legal implications of the AD's decision to allow some students to participate prior to completing their physical examinations? How are these legal ramifications related to the school's policy?

5. How is the physical examination problem likely to affect the organizational climate of the school's athletic department? How is it likely

to affect the relationship between the school and Dr. Mulligan? Between Dr. Mulligan and Steve Fu?

■ Application Exercise

How could this situation have been avoided? What would you have done if you were in Steve's position?

■ For background information on concepts presented in Case Study 19, see *Management Strategies in Athletic Training*, chapters 1, 2, and 8.

CASE STUDY 20

■ **Topic:** Developing educational program admission criteria

■ **Setting:** College athletic training educator

■ **Primary concept:** Ethics

■ **Secondary concept:** Policy and procedure development

The part of his job as curriculum director that Jarvis liked the least was trying to decide who should be admitted into the undergraduate athletic training major. There were always more qualified applicants than places in the program. Jarvis was almost always pleased with the students who were eventually admitted, but it was emotionally draining to have to tell a kid that he wasn't going to be admitted even though he was qualified. It was especially tough considering all the time Jarvis invested in recruiting applicants and grooming their interest in the college.

About a week after Jarvis mailed the acceptance and rejection letters to this year's candidates, the usual phone calls started to come in. Most rejected candidates and their parents were understanding, but this year there was one who was not ready to accept Jarvis's judgment in the matter. Rachel Buckwalter was a high school senior whose family members had attended the college since its founding in the early 1800s. Her grandfather was a past chairperson of the board of trustees. Her father was the CEO of the largest investment banking firm in the country. Rachel wanted to be an athletic trainer. She had been a successful athlete in high school, and following an injury and subsequent rehabilitation under the care of an athletic trainer she had decided that sports medicine would be her life's work. Her parents had discouraged her at first. They wanted her to study in a field that was more in keeping with the family's business interests and position among the power elite. Rachel had insisted, however, and eventually her parents relented.

Jarvis knew immediately after reviewing her application for the first time that Rachel would be unlikely to be admitted to the athletic training program. Her grades were marginal. In fact, she had been admitted to the college through the "Last Chance" program, which provided extra tutoring in a reduced course load for one semester. If students didn't achieve at a prescribed level after the trial semester, they were not readmitted for their sophomore year. In addition to her poor grades, Rachel's application essay was lousy. Jarvis decided to interview her anyway. The interview went poorly. Rachel could not articulate her reasons for wanting a career in athletic training. Her communication skills were poor. Total disaster. Jarvis eventually rejected her application in favor of someone who showed more promise and potential.

Rachel's mother didn't give Jarvis much of a chance to say anything during the telephone call. After hearing Jarvis's explanation for why Rachel's application had been denied, she launched into a 20-min tirade that included a specific threat to have Jarvis fired if he didn't admit Rachel to the program. Jarvis tried to explain that admitting Rachel into the program would mean denying a more worthy student the chance to participate. "You decide who's more worthy," she screeched, "someone whose family gives $100,000 a year to the college or some farm boy who doesn't belong here anyway." Then she hung up.

The next day Jarvis received a phone call from the president of the college. After hearing Jarvis's side of the story, he instructed Jarvis to admit Rachel Buckwalter into the athletic training program. "Jarvis," he explained, "I appreciate the great job you do, but I have to be concerned with the larger picture. I simply cannot afford to ignore the philanthropy of the Buckwalter family and what it means to this institution."

Jarvis was enraged that he was being forced to compromise his principles. He told himself he would have to think about this for a while before deciding what to do about Rachel Buckwalter.

∎ Analysis Questions

1. With what you know about the process Jarvis uses to admit students to the program, identify any aspects that predispose it to the kind of problem he now faces. What other kinds of problems might he eventually face under the present system? How could he change the system to avoid those problems?

2. Who has power in this case? How is it being used? Does Jarvis have any power? How can he exercise it most effectively?

3. What alternative actions could Jarvis take in light of the president's directive to admit Rachel Buckwalter to the program? What are the potential risks and benefits of each of these alternatives?

4. Assuming that Rachel is eventually admitted into the program, how should Jarvis handle what is likely to be a tense and difficult relationship to keep his problems from escalating?

■ Application Exercise

Develop an application process for an undergraduate athletic training major. Be sure to include the minimum standards, if any, for admission. Provide a rationale for each admission standard. Include any forms or instruments used in the application process.

■ For background information on concepts presented in Case Study 20, see *Management Strategies in Athletic Training*, chapters 1 and 2.

CASE STUDY 21

■ **Topic:** Student-athlete pregnancy policies

■ **Setting:** College

■ **Primary concept:** Policy and procedure development

■ **Secondary concepts:** Legal liability
Ethics

Kim DeLong was the athletic trainer at St. Ignatius Women's College. Two weeks ago students and faculty at the small, NCAA Division II school had been shocked to learn that one of the members of the basketball team was pregnant. What was even more disconcerting to some of the college community was that the player had decided to remain on the team throughout the season. She needed the partial athletic scholarship to stay in school. She didn't want to quit, even though some of the faculty and administration were pressuring her to do so. She intended to keep the baby once it was born. To many at this conservative academy, the whole affair was sordid and scandalous.

One day soon after the news of the pregnancy broke, Kim was summoned to the office of the vice president for student affairs, who also doubled as the athletic director. "Kim," she began, "I'm not sure there's much we can do about this case, but I'm upset that we weren't better prepared for it. We should have seen this coming. I want to be ready to deal with a pregnancy more effectively next time. Draft a policy statement that deals with pregnant student-athletes. You're our medical person and so I'm relying on your good judgment."

Kim consulted with her team physician and then drafted the following policy:

St. Ignatius Women's College
Student-Athlete Pregnancy Policy

The NCAA guideline for participation by a pregnant student-athlete will be used as the college's basic policy.

A student-athlete who is pregnant must inform the team physician or head athletic trainer of her condition as soon as it is confirmed. This is necessary so appropriate medical and emotional support can be made available as the student-athlete makes her decision. The team physician and the head athletic trainer will keep the student's condition confidential.

The student must receive appropriate prenatal counseling, and the team physician or specialist and the head athletic trainer must discuss with the student-athlete her medical condition and the risk of injury to both her and the fetus.

Only after counseling and discussion has occurred will the physician, in consultation with the head coach, student-athlete, and athletic administration, determine if the pregnant student-athlete will be permitted to compete.

Should the athlete choose to continue participation, she must properly execute a document of understanding and waiver before she is permitted to resume play.

The team physician or specialist will determine whether or not the student-athlete is cleared to return to participation following her pregnancy. If the student-athlete is not medically cleared by the physician to return to competition, she will receive permanent medical hardship classification. Guidelines governing permanent medical hardship will be discussed in detail with the student-athlete at the appropriate time.

The student-athlete, at any time, may choose not to continue participating on the team without jeopardizing her athletic scholarship for the length of the award period. If the student-athlete chooses not to continue competing, her athletic aid will not be renewed following the existing award period.

A student-athlete will not forfeit her team membership status, benefits, or responsibilities, nor be excluded from team activities due to pregnancy.

A student-athlete's pregnancy, childbirth, false pregnancy, termination of pregnancy, and recovery therefrom for so long as is deemed necessary by the team physician or specialists will be treated as a "medical hardship" or "leave of absence."

> *At the conclusion of the pregnancy the student-athlete shall be reinstated to the status she held when the leave began,*
>
> ### OR
>
> *If the student-athlete is medically cleared by the team physician to return to competition, she may participate on the team and receive one semester of athletic aid. Renewal of athletic aid will be in accordance with NCAA bylaw 15.3.5.*

A week after Kim submitted the policy to the vice president for student affairs, she received a phone call. "Take the clauses referring to 'her decision' and 'termination of pregnancy' out of this policy," ordered the VP. "This is a Christian institution and we will not condone even the suggestion of abortion on our campus. The rest of the policy is fine, but clean up this abortion-related language immediately. I'm surprised that you included it in the first place!"

▌ Analysis Questions

1. Does the document that Kim developed meet all the tests to be considered a policy? If not, how would you classify the document? Why is it important?

2. What medical flaws, if any, can be found in Kim's "policy?" What procedural flaws?

3. Is Kim's policy consistent with the body of case law on the rights of disabled students to participate in school-sponsored activities? Should pregnancy be treated differently than other medical conditions? Why or why not? Does St. Ignatius need a pregnancy policy? Why or why not?

4. Does the clause requiring a waiver adequately protect the college against lawsuits? Why or why not?

5. If you were in Kim's position, how willing would you be to remove the clauses that were so offensive to the vice president? In your opinion, should they remain in the policy? Why or why not?

6. If you wanted to leave the pregnancy termination clauses in the policy, what allies and strategies would you employ? What are the risks? What are the benefits?

■ Application Exercise

Devise a policy with supporting procedures on pregnant student-athletes. Submit it to a panel of fellow students acting as trustees of your institution. Allow the "trustees" to interview you regarding the proposed policy. Have the "trustees" vote on the policy.

■ For background information on concepts presented in Case Study 21, see *Management Strategies in Athletic Training*, chapters 1, 2, and 8.

CASE STUDY 22

∎ **Topic:** Power struggles and the chain of command

∎ **Setting:** High school

∎ **Primary concept:** Policy and procedure development

∎ **Secondary concepts:** Human resources
Communication
Legal liability

It had happened again after the game last night. Sherry Taft, the athletic trainer at Franklin High School, was becoming very frustrated. She had worked hard to convince the new orthopedic surgeon in her small town to become the school's team physician. Unfortunately, the football coach had a college friend who was an orthopedic surgeon at the university hospital in a city 50 miles away. Twice during the past week the coach had gone over Sherry's head to call the parents of injured players to strongly suggest that they seek their medical care from his friend at the university. Sherry was concerned that eventually she would lose her team physician because of the problem.

When the team physician called Sherry at home on Saturday afternoon, she knew she had trouble. "Sherry," the orthopedist began, "why didn't Ron Jones show up at my office this morning? I made a special appointment with him to examine the knee he injured in the game last night. He's the third kid in two weeks who has missed a special appointment. What's going on?" Sherry reluctantly decided to tell the surgeon about the football coach's intervention in the last three cases. Although she was apologetic and obviously frustrated about the situation, the doctor became upset when he heard the story. He told her that under the circumstances, he would no longer serve as the team physician for the school. Sherry begged him to reconsider and promised to confront the coach and even bring the matter to the AD if necessary, but the doctor held firm.

Sherry immediately placed a phone call to the football coach. Angrily she told him what had just transpired and demanded that he do something to rectify the situation. "Calm down, Sherry," he told her. "We don't need him anyway. My friend at the university is a better doctor and he's willing to see our athletes in his office whenever we want, so what's the problem?" Sherry was quick to tell him exactly what the problem was. The coach simply told her to get herself under control and they would talk about it on Monday.

▌ Analysis Questions

1. Sherry and the coach obviously have different perceptions about the role that a team physician should play in a school-based sports medicine program. What role do you think a team physician in this setting should play? Is it improper for the coach to suggest to parents that they seek medical treatment at the university hospital? Why or why not?

2. What problems does Sherry face now that she lacks a team physician? What services, normally provided by a team physician, will now be missing from her program? How will the school's legal liability exposure be affected?

3. To a significant degree, Sherry has allowed the coach to shape an important aspect of her sports medicine program. Who has power in this scenario? How has it been used? How could it be used to affect future outcomes? Who has authority? How can it be tapped to improve the situation?

▌ Application Exercise

How could this situation have been avoided? (What actions should Sherry have taken before receiving the phone call from the team physician that might have helped avoid the problem?) Develop policies and procedures to avoid this kind of conflict.

▌ For background information on concepts presented in Case Study 22, see *Management Strategies in Athletic Training*, chapters 1, 2, 3, and 8.

CASE STUDY 23

■ **Topic:** Establishing a scope of responsibility

■ **Setting:** Clinical

■ **Primary concept:** Policy and procedure development

■ **Secondary concepts:** Program planning and evaluation
Legal liability
Financial management

As part of Community Hospital's new quality assurance program, vice presidents were personally interviewing every staff member under their jurisdiction to determine ways to improve the hospital. John Duncan was the vice president for outpatient services, a division that was responsible for generating a significant percentage of the hospital's annual operating budget. As part of his interviewing schedule, he arranged to speak with each member of the physical therapy department, including Martha Williams, an athletic trainer who had worked in the department for 3 years.

Martha told John she was fairly satisfied with the way the department operated and particularly liked the fact that there was less bureaucracy than there had been at the clinic she used to work for. She enjoyed having her own caseload and being able to make her own decisions about patient care in consultation with the referring physicians. The one thing that bothered her, however, was that she thought the new department head viewed her in less favorable terms than the PTs she worked with. Martha told John that she had a good one-on-one relationship with each of the PTs, but that the new director seemed to want to establish a "pecking order." When the interview was finished, John thanked her for her time and honesty.

Six months later the hospital issued a report that contained new procedures to help improve the quality of care. Among the procedures that applied to the physical therapy department were the following:

- *All progress and discharge notes dictated by an athletic trainer shall be countersigned by a physical therapist.*
- *All athletic trainers, physical therapy assistants, and physical therapy aides shall carry out their duties under the* direct *supervision of a physical therapist.*
- *Only physical therapists shall conduct initial patient evaluations. Athletic trainers may conduct follow-up evaluations, but only under the supervision of a physical therapist.*

When Martha saw the directives her heart sank. For the past 3 years Community Hospital had been a great place to work. She had felt fulfilled both personally and professionally. Now it seemed that this job was about to become much like the one from which she thought she had escaped.

▌ Analysis Questions

1. Do the new procedures initiated by the hospital adequately support the policy of improved health care delivery for patients? Is patient care likely to be improved? Why or why not?

2. Are the new procedures consistent with the law governing the practice of medicine, physical therapy, and athletic training in your state? Why or why not?

3. What are the implications for third-party billing in this case? Do the new procedures support the practices normally associated with third-party billing in your state?

4. What is the likely effect of the new procedures on department members' commitment to accomplishing the mission of the department? How will the PTs be affected? How will the ATCs be affected?

5. What actions, if any, would you take if you were in Martha's position? What are the possible benefits of such actions? What are the risks?

▮ Application Exercise

Develop procedures for patient initial assessment, treatment, and discharge for a sports medicine clinic. Be sure to describe the setting in which your clinic exists (i.e., hospital versus private practice). Defend your procedures in the following terms:

- Legal defensibility
- Financial prudence
- Organizational soundness

▮ For background information on concepts presented in Case Study 23, see *Management Strategies in Athletic Training*, chapters 1, 2, 3, 6, 7, and 8.

CASE STUDY 24

■ **Topic:** The athletic trainer and prescription drugs

■ **Setting:** College

■ **Primary concept:** Legal liability

■ **Secondary concepts:** Policy and procedure development
Ethics

Although Toby Ellison was usually too busy to see injured athletes from the local high schools, he agreed to take a look at Rodney Simpson's knee injury. Rodney was the son of the county prosecutor who was a good friend of Toby's boss, the head football coach at the university. Under the circumstances Toby wasn't sure how he could refuse.

Rodney arrived at the university's main training room at noon. His dad had picked him up at school during his lunch break. Midway through the examination of Rodney's knee injury, Toby excused himself to answer the phone. "That's right," Toby said to the caller, "2,000 ibuprofen— make sure they are the 800 mg strength—and 1,000 of that new antibiotic. When will they be delivered? OK—sounds good. Thanks." Toby hung up the phone and returned to his examination of Rodney's knee. As Toby continued his exam, Mr. Simpson became concerned about the telephone conversation he had just overheard. "Was Toby ordering prescription drugs?" he asked himself. Because he had only caught bits and pieces of the conversation he decided to leave the issue alone for the moment.

Three weeks later Rodney and his dad were sitting in the front-row seats at the 50-yd line that the university football coach had provided for the big game against the conference rivals. The seats gave them a fantastic view of both the field and the players' bench area. During the game Mr.

Simpson clearly saw Toby Ellison reach into a trunk, pull out a bottle of pills, and give some to a player who appeared to be suffering from a painful injury. The memory of Toby's phone call 3 weeks ago was still fresh in his mind. He decided that if Toby was involved in distributing prescription drugs, he would be forced to investigate.

On Monday he called his friend, the coach, to thank him for the tickets. "While I've got you on the phone," Mr. Simpson said, "let me ask you—does Toby Ellison hand out prescription drugs in the training room?" Mr. Simpson could feel the wall of caution that surrounded the coach's response. "Toby only gives out those medicines when our doctor tells him to," replied the coach. "Besides, he doesn't keep any strong drugs around—just antiinflammatories and a few other things. That's the way it's done everywhere." Mr. Simpson thanked him again for the tickets and hung up. After calling a few of the players and asking them the same questions, he finally decided what he had to do.

A week later, the county sheriff walked into the training room, impounded all the prescription drugs in the locker in Toby's office, and served Toby with a summons to appear before the local judge on charges of illegal possession of controlled substances, practicing medicine without a license, and practicing pharmacy without a license.

▋ Analysis Questions

1. Toby's actions were not inconsistent with the way that prescription medicines are handled in training rooms all over the country. If Toby practiced in your state, would his actions have been illegal? Why or why not?

2. To whom should Toby turn to help him defend himself in this situation? If the case eventually goes to court, what expert witnesses might he call upon? What testimony would he want them to provide?

▋ Application Exercise

Develop a policy, with supporting processes and procedures, that addresses the use of prescription and nonprescription drugs in the university sports medicine program. As an appendix to the policy, attach the appropriate sections of the laws in your state that address this issue.

▋ For background information on concepts presented in Case Study 24, see *Management Strategies in Athletic Training*, chapters 2 and 8.

CASE STUDY 25

▌ Topic: Handling contraindicated patient prescriptions

▌ Setting: Clinical

▌ Primary concept: Ethics

▌ Secondary concepts: Human resources
Legal liability

The reception for the new orthopedic surgeon, hosted by his two retirement-age partners, was a big event in the medical community. Most of the town's 20 physicians attended the welcoming party for the young doctor, fresh from his residency at the state university hospital. Colin Jones, ATC, was pleased that he and his physical therapist boss had also been invited. Colin worked in the local hospital physical therapy department and served as the athletic trainer for both the high school and the local small college. He had high hopes for the new orthopedist. He was anxious to get him involved as a team physician for at least one of the programs he served. The older doctors had served for many years, but Colin felt they were a little too conservative. He wanted a physician who would treat athletes aggressively so they could return to practice and competition at the earliest possible moment.

As the reception was breaking up, Colin approached the new doctor and asked him if he would be willing to become involved as a team physician for one of the schools. The doctor told Colin that he thought that would be great, but he would have to check with his partners before committing himself. He told Colin that he would call him in a few days with an answer.

Two days later Colin passed the new doctor in the hallway of the hospital and asked him if he had spoken with his partners about the team physician issue yet. "I walked into a bit of a hornet's nest on that one," he replied. "I had no idea that my partners were so attached to their role as team physicians. I almost felt as if they sensed I was trying to force them out and take their place. Well, I managed to smooth it over, but I think I better hold off on any formal involvement with the school's athletic programs until my partners are ready to give it up. I'll still see plenty of the athletes, but the formal responsibilities of team physician will have to wait."

A week later Colin received his first referral from the new doctor. The patient was a 40-year-old runner who had slipped on some loose gravel. In falling, he had twisted his knee and torn his anterior cruciate ligament. The doctor had reconstructed the knee using the central third of the patellar tendon as a graft. Colin was confused by the prescription for therapy. Besides the typical orders related to range of motion and strengthening exercises, the doctor had specifically requested that Colin administer diathermy treatments. Colin was concerned about this aspect of the prescription because he assumed that the graft was being partially held in place with either a staple or a screw, which would be selectively heated during a diathermy treatment, causing an internal burn. Colin showed the prescription to his PT supervisor who told him to call the doctor to clarify the orders. When Colin finally reached the doctor by phone, he asked him about the diathermy order and explained his concerns. The doctor told Colin that he had seen this procedure used several times during his residency and that no negative side effects had been noticed. He told Colin not to worry and to implement the prescription as written.

Colin was becoming very concerned that he was not getting off to a good start with this new doctor for whom he had such high hopes.

▌ Analysis Questions

1. If you were in Colin's position, would you have handled the team physician request differently? Why or why not?

2. What are the possible side effects of the way in which Colin approached the team physician issue?

3. If you were in Colin's position and faced with a physician's order that you knew was contraindicated, what alternative actions could you take? What are the likely consequences of each of these actions?

∎ Application Exercise

How would you differentiate between orders that you are certain are contraindicated as opposed to those about which you are less certain? How would your actions be different, if at all, for each category of problem?

∎ For background information on concepts presented in Case Study 25, see *Management Strategies in Athletic Training*, chapters 3 and 8.

CASE STUDY 26

∎ **Topic:**   Developing records systems

∎ **Setting:**   Clinical

∎ **Primary concept:**   Information management

∎ **Secondary concepts:**   Human resources
Policy and procedure development
Financial management

Kate Dwyer's dreams were finally coming true. After working for nearly 10 years as an athletic trainer and physical therapist in a collegiate setting, she was finally setting out on her own and opening her own sports medicine clinic. Although she knew she would still be working long hours and that her job would be no less demanding, she was confident that the increased sense of control she would experience would make it all worthwhile.

Kate was worried about a few things, however. Her biggest concern was staffing. Kate was cautious and conservative by nature, and she didn't feel she could hire any staff until she had a better sense for what her personnel needs would be and how she was going to be able to pay for those needs.

For the first few weeks Kate tried to do everything herself. She treated patients, transcribed her own dictation, and filed insurance claims. Finally she came to the conclusion that she had to hire a medical office secretary, at least on a part-time basis. She contacted a personnel agency and within a few days had a secretary who worked 20 hours a week.

After about a month Kate's secretary came to her and asked if they could talk. "Kate," the secretary began, "I've been working here about a month now and I really like my job and I like you too. I don't want to complain, but there is just too much work for me to get done in the 20 hours I spend here each week. The biggest problem is all the dictation you want me to transcribe and file. It takes so much time that I'm starting to fall behind on other things like filing insurance claims. I'm afraid that is going to start costing you in the near future unless we can do something about it. Kate, I really don't want to work any more hours than I do now. My kids are still young and I want to be with them as much as I can. I guess what I'm asking is whether you might consider either hiring an additional part-time secretary or changing your medical records system.''

Kate was sympathetic to her secretary's request. During the past month they had formed a good relationship and Kate didn't want to lose her. On the other hand, she couldn't afford to add another secretary. She wondered what alternatives to her present medical records system she might employ.

▌ Analysis Questions

1. What are the potential problems associated with allowing Kate's secretary to fall behind in any of her areas of responsibility?

2. What medical records or patient charting alternatives could Kate consider? What are the advantages and disadvantages of each? How would they either compound or alleviate the problems associated with the present narrative dictation system?

3. Would the introduction of a computerized system be likely to improve the situation in Kate's office? How would it improve? Would it make the situation worse? How? Why?

▌ Application Exercise

Even if Kate doesn't completely abandon her narrative charting methods, she will still require a variety of forms to track the information required for her patient records. Develop a set of forms appropriate for this setting. Be sure to design a form for every patient-charting activity Kate is likely to need. Organize your forms into a booklet for future reference.

▌ For background information on concepts presented in Case Study 26, see *Management Strategies in Athletic Training*, chapter 6.

CASE STUDY 27

∎ **Topic:** Insurance fraud

∎ **Setting:** Clinical

∎ **Primary concept:** Ethics

∎ **Secondary concepts:** Information management
Legal liability
Financial management

Lisa Beltran was the director of athletic training services at the Sports Medicine Clinic of the West. SMCW was a large medical practice, owned by physicians, that housed its own radiology, laboratory, and outpatient therapy departments. One day while Lisa was waiting to begin her first session with a new patient, the department receptionist came to her and informed her that there could be an insurance problem with this case. The patient, Jerome Sullivan, was from one of the local high schools and had no personal insurance. His high school did have an excess policy, but the receptionist was sure that there was a 1-year limit on the payment of all claims and the doctor's notes in the file indicated that this injury occurred 13 months ago. She doubted whether Jerome, in fact, would be covered by any insurance plan for this injury.

Lisa thanked the receptionist for the information and called Jerome from the waiting room. Jerome crutched back to the treatment area and Lisa asked him to explain the circumstances of his injury. The information Jerome provided confirmed what the receptionist had told her.

After Jerome had completed his session and left, Lisa walked upstairs to discuss Jerome's insurance problem with Dr. Nolan, who told Lisa he was very familiar with Jerome's case. He also told Lisa that he was a close friend of the athletic director at Jerome's high school and that he was sure the AD would want the insurance company to pay for the injury so the school wouldn't be left holding the bill. He instructed Lisa to go back into Jerome's files and postdate the notes and injury date to conform with the 1-year insurance coverage period. He told her not to worry—this kind of thing happened all the time with "these crazy sports insurance policies."

Lisa did as Dr. Nolan instructed. Afterward, however, she had a nagging feeling that she had made the wrong decision.

∎ Analysis Questions

1. Was Lisa's decision to comply with Dr. Nolan's instructions ethical? Why or why not?
2. What are the legal ramifications of Lisa's actions?
3. If you were in Lisa's position, how would you have acted in this situation? What alternatives to Lisa's actions exist? What are the advantages and disadvantages to each of these actions?

∎ Application Exercise

Research the three-party billing laws in your state. The State Insurance Commission is a good place to start. Try to find answers to the following questions:

- Who can bill insurance companies for sports medicine related services?
- Under what circumstances can athletic trainers bill insurance companies for their services?
- What penalties exist in your state for insurance fraud?
- What procedures must clinicians follow in order to be reimbursed by insurance companies?

∎ For background information on concepts presented in Case Study 27, see *Management Strategies in Athletic Training*, chapter 7.

CASE STUDY 28

■ **Topic:** Using technology to enhance communication

■ **Setting:** College

■ **Primary concept:** Communication

■ **Secondary concepts:** Policy and procedure development
Information management
Legal liability
Ethics

As far as the coaching staff at State Technological University was concerned, they had the best athletic training program in the conference, if not the country. In their opinion, Janelle Damson, Tech's certified athletic trainer, had built a remarkable program since coming to the university nearly 8 years ago. They especially appreciated her willingness and ability to communicate with them. The coaches felt good about the fact that Janelle kept them up to date on the health and participation status of their athletes on a daily basis.

Janelle was the only certified athletic trainer at the university. Although she had a cadre of students to assist her, she knew that her success or failure would be determined by her ability to organize the program with maximum efficiency. One area of concern was the manner in which Janelle communicated with coaches regarding the health and participation status of their student-athletes. During Janelle's first few years at Tech, she had laboriously handwritten 18 injury reports—one for each team—every day. She then had to walk up two floors to the athletic office, make copies of the reports, and place them in each coach's mailbox by 11:00 a.m. each day. The process took about 1 hour to complete. A few years ago Janelle received a computer for the training room. With the help of a computer science student who played on the basketball team, Janelle developed a computerized version of the daily injury report she had been using. The computerized process allowed her to greatly reduce the amount of information she had to enter on the form because the computer automatically retrieved the participation status data from the previous day's report. All Janelle had to do was type in the new injuries and edit yesterday's participation status list. Even with the new system, however, Janelle still had to copy the forms and distribute them by hand. The process still took about half an hour.

Janelle had an idea for reducing the amount of time spent on the process even further. Since all the coaches now had computers in their offices that were connected to the university's mainframe, why not find a way to send the daily injury report by electronic mail? Using E-mail would allow the coaches to access all the information they needed regarding the health and participation status of their athletes, while saving Janelle valuable time she could put to more productive use. The university president had directed all departments to investigate the possible uses of electronic mail as a way to decrease the flow of paper on campus. This seemed like a logical way to comply with that directive. And the coaches wouldn't even have to leave their desks and walk to the mail room to get the information.

Janelle worked with the campus computer center for nearly a month before the system was finally ready to go. With one keystroke, Janelle was able to send all the day's reports to their respective coaches. The entire process, from entering the data to sending it through the E-mail system, now took about 10 min—for all 18 sports! Janelle was very pleased with herself.

Most of the coaches adapted well to the system. Janelle had gone to great lengths to provide the coaches with the training they needed to use the system. She made up instruction cards and taped them to their computers. She met with each coach to explain how the system worked. She thought she had done everything possible to make the coaches comfortable. All the coaches liked the system except for John Mitchell, who had been the wrestling coach for nearly 30 years. The computer the university had provided for him had never been turned on. Coach Mitchell was uncomfortable with any new technology—he still had trouble operating his VCR. Janelle was determined to make her new system work for Coach Mitchell, but no matter how hard she tried, he refused to adapt to it. When he asked Janelle to provide him with a written report as she had in the past, Janelle refused. She knew that if she continued to provide him with written reports he would never learn the new system. Besides, she didn't want to establish a precedent for giving some coaches written reports and some electronic mail reports. That would defeat the purpose for which she had developed the new system—increased efficiency.

During Janelle's annual performance review, the AD told her she wasn't communicating well enough with some coaches. She was upset and honestly didn't know what else she could do.

▌Analysis Questions

1. What alternative actions should Janelle have considered to improve the injury reporting system? What are the advantages and disadvantages of each of these alternatives?

2. What problems might Janelle's new system create? Are these problems adequately offset by the increased efficiency Janelle now enjoys? Why or why not?

3. What are the legal implications of communicating with coaches about the health status of their athletes given the laws and ethics governing patient-practitioner confidentiality? Does the athletic trainer have the same kind of relationship with an athlete as a physician has with a patient? Why or why not?

4. Should Janelle be concerned about the confidentiality of the information she shares with coaches, especially in the context of an electronic system?

5. Would you have complied with Coach Mitchell's request for a written report? Why or why not?

▌Application Exercise

The switch to new technology can be difficult for some. Develop an educational program to help Janelle's coaches learn, understand, and accept her E-mail injury report idea. Use your institution's E-mail system as a model for the program you develop. Be sure to include any educational materials you think are appropriate.

▌For background information on concepts presented in Case Study 28, see *Management Strategies in Athletic Training*, chapters 6 and 8.

CASE STUDY 29

■ **Topic:** Marketing clinical sports medicine services

■ **Setting:** Clinical

■ **Primary concept:** Program planning and evaluation

■ **Secondary concept:** Financial management

The sports medicine business in the metro area was becoming increasingly competitive. Since he joined Total Rehabilitation Services 2 years ago as the company's first certified athletic trainer, Brad Fink had seen four new clinics established within 5 mi of the TRS main facility. The presence of these new clinics was definitely being felt at TRS. Referrals were down by nearly 30% from the previous year, and Brad was concerned that if things didn't change soon, he might lose his job because of the business slump.

When Brad arrived at work on Monday there was a note on his desk asking him to report to Susan Fletcher, one of the owners of TRS. Brad had a break between his first two patients and strolled down to Susan's office then. "Come on in, Brad!" welcomed Susan. "Brad, you have been one of the strongest advocates in the company for shifting at least part of our resources into the sports medicine market. Although I have agreed with you, the other partners weren't ready to commit the resources. With the recent business downturn, however, I think they have finally realized that we simply must become more competitive or we will be forced to continue handing patients over to the other clinics in town. Brad, I want to be able to make a proposal at the next partners' meeting in 3 weeks that TRS launch a comprehensive program of sports medicine services targeted at both high school and adult recreational athletes. To be successful, however, I need your help. You understand these markets better than I do. I want you to develop a comprehensive marketing plan for the new program. Keep in mind that we probably won't hire any new staff until the program has proven its ability to generate revenue. I've arranged to have your patient load reduced by half for the next 3 weeks so you can devote time to this project. I'm sure you'll have questions from time to time, so don't hesitate to call on me for help. Brad, I don't need to tell you how important this is both to you and the company. Thanks for helping me with it.''

This was the most excited Brad had been since coming to TRS. "Finally," he thought, "I'm going to have the chance to be an athletic trainer and do the work I was trained to instead of acting like a second-rate hired hand around here.''

▌ Analysis Questions

1. What information does Brad need before he can develop a marketing plan? After deciding what questions he should ask, invent plausible answers as if you were in Susan Fletcher's position. Keep in mind that the central purpose of the program is to boost the clinic's competitiveness and thereby generate increased revenue.

2. To whom would you market the new sports medicine program if you were in Brad's position? Who would be the primary audience for your marketing effort? Who would be the secondary audience?

3. What techniques would you use to market the program? What evidence exists, if any, to justify the use of these techniques? How do you know they will be effective?

▌ Application Exercise

Develop a complete marketing plan for the program using the parameters you provided in question 1. After describing the elements of the marketing plan, use either the PERT or Gannt techniques to develop a suggested time line for implementation of the plan. Then, develop a line-item budget for the marketing plan.

▌ For background information on concepts presented in Case Study 29, see *Management Strategies in Athletic Training*, chapters 2 and 4.

CASE STUDY 30

■ **Topic:** Personnel deployment

■ **Setting:** Clinical

■ **Primary concept:** Policy and procedure development

■ **Secondary concepts:** Human resources
Legal liability
Ethics

It started with little things. A 50-year-old factory worker with emphysema and a protruding disc. A grandmother with cervical pain of unknown etiology. Supervising cardiac patients during exercise therapy. All were problems that Gina Marosi, ATC, *thought* she could handle but with which she was neither very knowledgeable nor comfortable. She thought that when she finished graduate school and joined the staff at the clinic she would be working with patients with sports injuries. And although most of her cases were related in some way to sports, or at least orthopedics, it seemed that lately most of the sports injuries were being snapped up by the PTs. Most of these patients were highly motivated to get better, and it was understandable that their cases would be sought after. The clinic director had slowly but surely been assigning her to cases that she simply didn't feel qualified to handle.

One day when Gina checked the assignment board that listed her patients she saw that she was scheduled to supervise therapy for an 80-year-old stroke victim later that afternoon. "No way," Gina muttered to herself. "There is no way I'm going to take that patient. I don't know the first thing about CVA [cerebrovascular accident] rehab. Even though I've watched some of the PTs doing it with a few patients, that doesn't make me qualified.''

Gina walked over to the director's office and knocked. "Come in Gina," said the director. "What's on your mind this morning?" "You've scheduled me with a CVA patient this afternoon," Gina responded icily. "I can't take that patient. I don't have the training for it. I'm not qualified to work with those kinds of patients. I thought I was hired to work with sports-related injuries. Lately you've been giving most of those to the other staff members and shifting work my way that I'm not qualified to handle. Why?"

"Gina," said the director, "you have to understand my position, too. The PTs on the staff weren't wild about hiring an athletic trainer in the first place. Now don't get me wrong—now that you're here and they have gotten to know you they think it was a great idea. But they want some variety in the kind of patients they see. They were upset because you were getting all the 'good' patients. I'm simply trying to keep everybody as happy as possible. I'll tell you what I'll do. I'll reassign the CVA case if you're uncomfortable with it. But I suggest you spend some time looking over one of the PT's shoulders the next time we have a CVA case, because you're going to be carrying a more varied work load from now on."

Gina's heart sank as she walked back to the therapy area. After her talk with the director, she felt that she had been hired under false pretenses. "I guess I better check out a book on CVA therapy from the hospital library before I leave today," she thought.

▌Analysis Questions

1. What are the legal risks inherent in the director's case assignment practices?

2. Is Gina legally bound to accept cases for which she has had no training? Is she ethically bound? If so, why? If not, what standards should she use to decide which cases she should take and which she should refuse?

▌ Application Exercise

Place yourself in the director's position and construct a policy with supporting processes and procedures that governs the way patients are assigned to departmental staff in a typical sports medicine clinic. Make sure that all policies, processes, and procedures are consistent with your state's laws governing the practice of medicine, athletic training, and physical therapy.

▌ For background information on concepts presented in Case Study 30, see *Management Strategies in Athletic Training*, chapters 2, 3, and 8.

About the Author

Richard Ray is the head athletic trainer and an associate professor of physical education at Hope College in Holland, Michigan. He has directed the school's sports medicine program since 1982 and is a recognized leader in the field of athletic training administration. Ray received a BSEd in physical education from the University of Michigan in 1979, an MA in athletic training from Western Michigan University (WMU) in 1980, and an EdD in educational leadership from WMU in 1990. He graduated summa cum laude in both graduate programs and was honored as a Graduate Research and Creative Scholar by WMU in 1990.

Dr. Ray is the author of the book, *Management Strategies in Athletic Training*. In addition to being a member of the National Athletic Trainers Association (NATA), Ray is a member and past president of both the Great Lakes Athletic Trainers Association and the Michigan Athletic Trainers Society. He is also a member of the NATA Board of Certification Task Force on Examination Qualifications. In 1993 Ray was named to the Educational Advisory Board of the Gatorade Sport Science Institute. His favorite leisure activities include camping, reading, playing golf, and coaching summer youth sports.

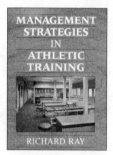